ICNC **MONOGRAPH** SERIES

SERIES EDITOR: Maciej Bartkowski
CONTACT: mbartkowski@nonviolent-conflict.org
VOLUME EDITORS: Amber French
DESIGNED BY: David Reinbold
CONTACT: icnc@nonviolent-conflict.org

Other volumes in this series:

The Power of Staying Put: Nonviolent Resistance against Armed Groups in Colombia, Juan Masullo (2015)

The Tibetan Nonviolent Struggle: A Strategic and Historical Analysis, Tenzin Dorjee (2015)

Published by ICNC Press
International Center on Nonviolent Conflict
1775 Pennsylvania Ave. NW. Ste. 1200
Washington, D.C. 20006 USA

© 2016 International Center on Nonviolent Conflict, Jonathan Pinckney
All rights reserved. ISBN: 978-1-943271-06-1

Cover Photos: (l) Ukraine Revolution blog, via Wikimedia Commons (r and Title Page) *A Force More Powerful* documentary.

A protester in Kyiv inserts roses into riot police shields in 2004 during the Orange Revolution.

In October 2010, protesters in West Papua demonstrate remarkable nonviolent discipline in their call for a referendum to grant independence from Indonesia.

African-American college students sit in at a downtown Nashville, Tennessee, lunch counter in 1960 to defy racial segregation.

Peer Review: This ICNC monograph underwent three blind peer reviews to be considered for publication. Scholarly experts in the field of civil resistance and related disciplines, as well as practitioners of nonviolent actions, serve as independent reviewers of the ICNC monograph manuscripts.

Publication Disclaimer: The designations used and material presented in this publication do not indicate the expression of any opinion whatsoever on the part of ICNC. The author holds responsibility for the selection and presentation of facts contained in this work, as well as for any and all opinions expressed therein, which are not necessarily those of ICNC and do not commit the organization in any way.

Making or Breaking Nonviolent Discipline

IN CIVIL RESISTANCE MOVEMENTS

Photo credit: Jonathan McIntosh/Wikimedia Commons

Summary

A central question in the study and practice of civil resistance is how nonviolent movements can maintain nonviolent discipline among their members. What factors encourage and sustain nonviolent discipline, particularly in the face of violent repression? While several scholars have suggested answers to these questions to date, the answers have largely remained *ad hoc* and have not been systematically tested. This monograph addresses these deficits in the literature by offering a unified theory of nonviolent discipline. This theory provides a helpful tool for better understanding how nonviolent discipline is created, sustained and shaped by repression. Following the theory, the monograph presents two tests of the effects of several influences on nonviolent discipline. The first is on the impact of patterns of repression, history of civil resistance, and campaign leadership and structure on nonviolent discipline. The second is a comparison of three civil resistance campaigns from the post-Communist "Color Revolutions" in Serbia, Georgia and Kyrgyzstan. Some of the central findings of these two tests include:

- Repression consistently lowers nonviolent discipline, reinforcing the need for campaigns to carefully strategize their responses to it.
- Nonviolent discipline also falls significantly following government concessions offered to resisters, possibly due to campaign over-confidence or movement splits.
- Non-hierarchical campaigns with observable internal debates, opposing schools of thoughts, and even conflicts are better at maintaining nonviolent discipline, suggesting that campaigns should be decentralized and work on building participant ownership over the campaign if they want to instill greater nonviolent discipline.

The study concludes with general and specific recommendations that inform further research, civil resistance practice and policy-making. The main recommendations include:

- For academics, greater research into the individual-level factors that sustain nonviolent discipline, particularly the quality of training, gender and the influence of peers.
- For civil resistance practitioners, building campaigns that do not necessarily rely on hierarchical structures but rather focus on consistent nonviolent messaging and building campaign ownership at an individual level.
- For policy-makers and members of civil society, supporting civil resistance through advocacy against repression, and providing support to civil resistance early in the campaign life cycle.

Table of Contents

Summary	5
Introduction	9
Chapter 1: Literature Review and Theory	13
Violence, Nonviolence, and Nonviolent Discipline	13
Sources of Nonviolent Discipline: Ethical and Strategic	18
Other Sources of Nonviolent Discipline	20
A Theory of Nonviolent Discipline	21
Expected Influences on Nonviolent Discipline	24
Chapter 2: Statistical Analysis and Results	35
Results of Statistical Tests	37
Chapter 3: Comparing the Color Revolutions	45
Serbia: Bulldozers Not Bullets	46
Georgia: Roses in Parliament	51
Kyrgyzstan: The Bloody Tulip	54
Chapter 4: Case Study Discussion	59
Historical Experience	59
Training and Information on Past Civil Resistance Campaigns	60
Wide Range of Past Civil Resistance Tactics	60
Previous Political Concessions	61
Appeals from Movement Leaders for Nonviolent Discipline	61
Strong, Cohesive Campaign Leadership	62
Moderate Strategic Goals	62
Tactical Choices to Avoid Confrontation	62
Membership Criteria Excluding Violent Actors	63
High Levels of Diversity	64
Campaign Punishment for Violent Actions	65
Repression of Nonviolent Action	65
Conclusion: Applied Learning on Nonviolent Discipline	69
Scholar-Relevant Findings	69
Activist-Relevant Findings	72
Findings for Civil Society and Policymakers	74
Appendix A: Statistical Annex	76
Results and Discussion	83
Cited Literature	90
Case Study References	97
List of Tables and Figures	100

Introduction[1]

In 1930 Mahatma Gandhi called on the people of India to engage in a massive campaign of civil disobedience against British rule. In particular the campaign targeted the colonial monopoly on the production of salt. Across the country, individuals broke the law against home production of salt, challenging the rightfulness of British rule. Yet perhaps one of the most powerful moments of the campaign took place not through salt production, but through the violent repression of peaceful activists. At the Dharasana Salt Works, followers of Gandhi attempted to peacefully occupy the facilities and shut down production. Soldiers at the facility refused to allow them to enter and brutally beat the nonviolent protesters as they marched towards the facility.

Yet, as powerfully recorded by the newspapers of the day and later depicted in Richard Attenborough's film *Gandhi*, despite these brutal attacks the protesters responded neither with violence nor with fear. Instead, peacefully yet determinedly, they continued to march forward, line after line, to be beaten. They refused to give in, yet they did not meet violence with violence. This violent repression became one of the most powerful moments of Gandhi's campaign for Indian independence, as the nonviolent discipline of the satyagrahis revealed the brutality of colonial rule and spoke powerfully to the justice of the Indian cause.

Thirty years later in Nashville, Tennessee, USA, a group of African-American students sat down at several "Whites Only" lunch counters and politely asked to be served lunch. Upon being denied, they quietly sat at the counter with their books and studied, not responding with anger or violence, but with a quiet determination to not give up the fight. Trained in earlier workshops to not respond to provocation, these students and many others continued this "nonviolent occupation" of lunch counters in Nashville

---

[1] The author would like to thank Maciej Bartkowski, Erica Chenoweth, Brian Martin, Hardy Merriman, Pauline Moore, and an anonymous reviewer for very helpful comments and discussion, as well as the International Center on Nonviolent Conflict for supporting this research.

and across the South. White patrons sought again and again to drive them out through violence and intimidation, hurling insults and epithets, and sometimes even engaging in direct physical violence such as aggressively pulling activists from the chairs down to the ground or putting lit cigarettes out on the lunch counter occupiers' bodies. Yet they remained calm, peaceful and nonviolent, never giving the authorities an excuse to expel them. Their quiet discipline and determination eventually led to the desegregation of lunch counters in Nashville, and was a crucial turning point in the larger Civil Rights Campaign against the racist oppression of the Jim Crow South.

In these well-known campaigns and many others across the globe, dedicated practitioners of nonviolent action have achieved transformative changes from fighting corruption (Beyerle 2014) to achieving national liberation (Bartkowski 2013), to overthrowing oppressive dictatorships (Chenoweth and Stephan 2011). Waves of primarily nonviolent movements such as those that overthrew the Communist regimes of Eastern Europe, the "Color Revolutions" of the early 2000s, or the "Arab Spring" movements of 2011 have demonstrated to the world the power of nonviolent resistance to successfully challenge entrenched autocratic rulers even in the most forbidding of environments.

Academic research has confirmed the effectiveness of nonviolent action. A long tradition beginning in the early 20th century pointed to the potential for nonviolent action to solve critical problems such as fighting injustice (Martin 2007), and even protecting countries against invasion (Roberts 1967, Boserup and Mack 1974). Many other scholars analyzed particular nonviolent movements (Zunes et al 1999, Roberts and Garton Ash 2009, Nepstad 2011), with important works on major campaigns such as the fight for Indian independence (Shridharani 1939), the U.S. Civil Rights Movement (McAdam 2010, Isaac et al 2012), the South African Anti-Apartheid Movement (Zunes 1999), the Palestinian Intifada (King 2009, Hallward 2013) and the campaign that ousted Serbian dictator Slobodan Milosevic (Binnendijk and Marovic 2006). More recently, a wave of statistical research into nonviolent action has been inspired by the finding from researchers Erica Chenoweth and Maria Stephan that nonviolent movements succeed roughly twice as often as their violent counterparts (Chenoweth and Stephan 2011).[2]

---

[2] This research has examined a number of important questions including the causes for the onset of civil resistance campaigns, factors encouraging success of civil resistance campaigns, and links between civil resistance and democracy. For some excellent examples of this recent research see: Braithwaite et al 2015, Butcher and Svensson 2014, Chenoweth and Ulfelder 2015, Gleditsch and Rivera 2015, and White et al 2015.

Introduction

One of the critical keys to the success of these movements has been what scholars have referred to as "nonviolent discipline." Like the satyagrahis at the Dharasana Salt Works or the students of the Nashville lunch counters, activists in many struggles have bravely remained firm and yet nonviolent, refusing to respond to violence with violence. This nonviolent discipline can "reveal the adversary's repressive measures in the harshest light" (King 2002), often sparking a process referred to by scholars as "backfire" (Hess and Martin 2006) or "political jiu-jitsu" (Sharp 1973). In this process, violent repression of nonviolent activists undermines the oppressor's legitimacy and demonstrates the justice of the nonviolent activists' cause. This in turn can undermine the oppressors' power by leading their supporters to no longer support them and instead support the cause of the nonviolent activists.

> *Without nonviolent discipline, regimes and their supporters often successfully paint activists' struggles as dangerous and disruptive, and ordinary people move to support their suppression.*

Without nonviolent discipline, regimes and their supporters often successfully paint activists' struggles as dangerous and disruptive, and ordinary people move to support their suppression. Even scattered incidents of violence can "crowd out" a largely nonviolent movement's impact and decrease participation in civil resistance (Sharp 1973; Chenoweth and Schock 2015; Day et al 2015). Because of these dynamics, activists and scholars of nonviolent action have nearly unanimously argued that nonviolent discipline is crucial to achieving success through nonviolent action (Popovic et al 2007, Ackerman and DuVall 2006, Nepstad 2011).

Where does such discipline come from? And how can movements encourage it? Transformative leaders of nonviolent resistance such as Mahatma Gandhi and James Lawson have extensively studied ways to encourage nonviolent discipline in their own movements. And writers on nonviolent action have offered many suggestions. Yet little careful academic study has been done to examine what factors consistently influence nonviolent discipline across a large number of nonviolent campaigns in different circumstances.

This monograph presents a unified theory of nonviolent discipline in civil resistance campaigns, drawing on arguments from the literature and a mathematical model. This theoretical framework, while intentionally simple and abstract, is a first cut at providing a systematic set of tools that academics, educators, activists and organizers

can use to understand the basic conditions that make nonviolent discipline easier or harder to create and sustain. After presenting the theory, the monograph proposes a set of expected influences that may affect nonviolent discipline.

While the theory's broad logic is applicable to political struggle in many different contexts with and without repression, this monograph focuses on anti-government campaigns in non-democracies with a political environment where repression is expected and violence often takes place on both sides. Since maintaining nonviolent discipline will be particularly challenging in these circumstances, understanding the factors that can nonetheless consistently promote it will be particularly important.

The monograph is divided into four sections. The first reviews some of the academic literature on nonviolent discipline as well as nonviolent action more broadly, and presents the monograph's own theoretical framework. The second tests the predictions of the theory of nonviolent discipline on a dataset of nearly 18,000 actions by anti-government campaigns in 14 countries from 1991 to 2012. The data for this statistical testing are drawn from the Nonviolent and Violent Campaigns and Outcomes (NAVCO) 3.0 dataset, a data collection project that gathers detailed information on the actions of violent and nonviolent anti-government campaigns. Because NAVCO 3.0 has detailed information on individual actions, it provides an ideal way of testing how and when nonviolent discipline breaks down or is maintained in civil resistance campaigns.[3]

The third section presents a structured, focused comparison of the "Color Revolutions" in Serbia, Georgia and Kyrgyzstan, three prominent cases of civil resistance campaigns with varying levels of nonviolent discipline. The final section presents a concise summary of the findings, their potential application for activists, organizers and policymakers, and directions for future research.

---

[3] Much more information on the structure, sources, and advantages of NAVCO 3.0 is included in the statistical appendix.

Chapter 1
Literature Review and Theory

Violence, Nonviolence, and Nonviolent Discipline

While nonviolent discipline is a concept used almost universally in the literature on civil resistance, different scholars have applied its specific meaning in varying ways. One reason for this variation is the contested nature of its related concepts of violence and nonviolence. As Boserup and Mack wrote in the 1970s: "There is no general agreement in the literature on the scope of the concept of non-violence." (Boserup and Mack 1974, 11). Douglas Bond also points to the challenging nature of defining "nonviolence" since the concept carries such powerful emotional and normative weight (Bond 1988). While academics and activists have developed an extensive literature on the subject in the decades since these writings,[4] contention over definitions of "violence" and "nonviolence" continues today (Martinez 2015, May 2015). These debates have been complex, and are far beyond the scope of this monograph to fully address. However, some brief words on "violence" and "nonviolence" are in order.

In regard to the definition of "violence," arguments from peace studies literature have pointed to the importance of looking beyond direct physical harm. One particularly influential definition comes from early peace scholar Johan Galtung. Galtung defined violence as "present when human beings are being influenced so that their actual somatic and mental realizations are below their potential realizations" (Galtung 1969, 168). The comprehensiveness and simplicity of Galtung's definition have made it an important touchstone.

Definitions of "nonviolence" similarly vary, from purely negative definitions revolving around refraining from physical violence to more expansive definitions that involve particular lifestyle commitments and attitudes towards others. Some thinkers

---

[4] On academic literature see for example Ackerman and DuVall 2000, Ackerman and Kruegler 1993, Helvey 2004, Nepstad 2011, Roberts and Garton Ash 2009, Schock 2005, Sharp 2005, Summy 1994, Zunes et al 1999, and many others.

parse this difference by contrasting "nonviolence" as a personal belief system with "nonviolent action" as an active method of political struggle (Schock 2005, May 2015).[5] Gandhi incorporated both of these aspects in his articulation of "negative" and "positive" ahimsa (Iyer 1973, 180), with the first referring to refraining from harm, while the second implied positive action motivated by love. Martin Luther King, Jr. described nonviolent resistance as "not only [avoiding] external physical violence but also internal violence of the spirit," and claimed that its goal was inherently to find reconciliation (King 1957). James Lawson, a foundational figure in spreading Gandhian ideals of nonviolent thought and actions to the US Civil Rights Movement, similarly argued that a mentality of forgiveness was at the heart of "nonviolence" (Isaac et al 2012).

In contrast, seminal scholar Gene Sharp defines nonviolent action simply as "a technique of socio-political action for applying power in a conflict without the use of violence" (Sharp 1999, 567); others following Sharp have articulated similar definitions (Schock 2005, Chenoweth and Stephan 2011). These are negative definitions in regard to violence, but also positive in the sense that they consider nonviolent action to be active, extra-institutional political contention. Doing nothing may be "non-violent" but it is emphatically not "nonviolent action" (Day et al 2015).

While recognizing the central importance of the definitions of "nonviolence" that incorporate these broader moral principles, and the crucial work done by moral and philosophical theorists such as Gandhi,[6] this monograph primarily operates on the more reduced definition proposed by Sharp.

Nonviolent pioneers such as Gandhi and the leaders of the US Civil Rights Movement recognized the importance of "discipline" in nonviolent action campaigns. In Gandhi's extensive writing this was related to the question of nonviolent action or satyagraha as part of a larger suite of personal self-disciplines (Gandhi 1999). The Civil Rights Movement, in part inspired by Gandhi, also placed heavy emphasis on nonviolent action being undertaken in a strict, disciplined manner so as to maximize the impact of members' actions and de-legitimize the violent repression used against the movement. Early theorists of nonviolent action such as Richard Gregg also spoke of the importance of "discipline" for nonviolent resistance but left its scope extremely broad and largely a

---

[5] This monograph largely takes this approach — referring to the broader set of ethical practices as "nonviolence," while using "nonviolent action" or "civil resistance" to refer to the technique of applying power in conflict without violence (Sharp 1999).

[6] Indeed, much of the very language that shapes the study of nonviolent action today has its source in Gandhi. For a discussion of this, see King 2014, 296.

matter of individual practices (Gregg 1935, 224-250).

Sharp, while perhaps one of the first to discuss "nonviolent discipline" as a concept in depth, similarly left its definition ambiguous. Sharp defines the term simply as "adherence to certain minimum standards of behavior" (Sharp 1973, 615). While it is clear from Sharp's larger discussion that these minimum standards include refraining from physical violence, he also includes other elements of adherence to the movement's goals in his discussion. They include, among others, willingness to participate in menial or repetitive tasks that organizing or even waging civil resistance might involve, and carefully following the direction of movement leaders. In this conceptualization, the emphasis in "nonviolent discipline" is on the discipline, with the nonviolent understood as an aspect of the broader concept of personal discipline in the service of a larger goal.

One explicit definition of nonviolent discipline that follows Sharp's emphasis comes from Mattaini, who defines it as "maintaining adherence to a minimum set of standards for behavior as a member of a nonviolent activist group" (Mattaini 2013, 104-5). As with Sharp, this definition emphasizes the discipline side: "standards for behavior" include refraining from physical violence, but also potentially a wide number of other factors such as following the strategic plans of campaign leaders and treating other campaign participants with respect and consideration.

In contrast, in much of the literature on civil resistance, the term "nonviolent discipline," while often left undefined, is used to mean refraining from physical violence. For example, this type of definition of nonviolent discipline is being used in discussions of "political jiu-jitsu" or "backfire," the phenomenon that connotes how repression of nonviolent campaigns turns back against the violent authority and negatively impacts the capabilities of the repressor (Hess and Martin 2006, Sutton et al 2014). In these works the emphasis is on the nonviolent, with the discipline simply denoting consistency of behavior.

How can we describe and measure whether a campaign of nonviolent action possesses nonviolent discipline? The simplest approach is a straightforward "either/or" framework. Civil resistance campaigns can be described as having "maintained" or "failed to maintain" nonviolent discipline. Yet as organizers, practitioners and activist-intellectuals know well, applying this simple "present or absent" division to civil resistance campaigns as a whole has problems in the real world.

The biggest problem with a simple "either/or" definition of nonviolent discipline is that the boundary for crossing from "maintaining" to "not maintaining" nonviolent

discipline unclear. Completely refraining from any kind of violence by all participants in the campaign is an extremely challenging standard. If a single instance of physical violence disqualifies a campaign from being nonviolent, then the number of major civil resistance campaigns that have maintained nonviolent discipline throughout their entire period of struggle is exceptionally low. Yet beyond this absolute standard it is difficult to devise a clear and logical standard for "maintaining" nonviolent discipline that is not arbitrary. Thus, instead of using an arbitrary "present of absent" definition of nonviolent discipline, this study uses a more complex framework which starts at the individual campaign participant and then moves to the larger campaign.

For the individual, the monograph defines nonviolent discipline as refraining from the use of physical violence or the threat of physical violence directed at persons or property. In one sense this is a yes or no definition: any level of physical violence represents a violation of individual nonviolent discipline. Yet gradations in the intensity of violence at the individual level are also relevant, and when analyzing violations of nonviolent discipline, this monograph attempts to apply reasonable standards of relative intensity of violence. Both breaking a window at a demonstration and shooting a policeman with a handgun are individual-level violations of nonviolent discipline, but the second would be considered a much larger and more consequential violation constituting a more significant breakdown in a nonviolent discipline.[7]

For the civil resistance campaign[8] this monograph defines the level of nonviolent discipline by aggregating these individual decisions to refrain from or engage in physical violence. As the number of individuals in a campaign who engage in violence increases and their violent acts increase in frequency and intensity, a campaign's nonviolent discipline decreases. By this definition, nonviolent discipline is something that is rarely (if ever) fully present or fully absent. Instead, campaigns have higher or lower levels of

---

[7] Among practitioners and theorists of civil resistance there is significant debate over so-called "gray areas" between violent and nonviolent resistance. Some do not consider property damage, for instance, to be violent resistance. Many in the Palestinian struggle for statehood have also argued that throwing stones is not "violent" since it does not involve the use of weapons and has very little possibility of actually harming the Israeli soldiers at whom it is typically directed – its "violence" is primarily a form of visceral symbolic protest. While these debates are certainly worth having, this monograph operates on a simpler, more empirical definition, recognizing that even actions with minimal actual harm may be perceived as harmful and threatening. For good examples of discussion over these more ambiguous areas of "violence," see Boserup and Mack 1974, 40-44 and Sharp 1973, 608-11. For discussion specifically of stone throwing in the Palestinian movement, see Hallward 2013 and King 2009.

[8] This study examines civil resistance "campaigns" – defined, following Ackerman and Kruegler (1993) and Chenoweth and Stephan, as: "a series of observable, continual tactics in pursuit of a political objective," Chenoweth and Stephan 2011, 14.

nonviolent discipline depending on a large number of individual campaign participant decisions. Campaigns sometimes have "very high" nonviolent discipline when the vast majority of participants remain nonviolent. They sometimes have "low" nonviolent discipline when the campaign as a whole remains generally nonviolent but with many individual instances of violence.

This monograph follows the practice of several major works on nonviolent action (Ackerman and Kruegler 1993, Chenoweth and Stephan 2011) in limiting the population of civil resistance campaigns to those campaigns of resistance that "primarily" engage in nonviolent tactics.[9] At a certain point as the proportion of individuals in a campaign that participate in violent action increases and the intensity and frequency of their violent actions similarly increase, it becomes no longer meaningful to refer to a campaign as one "primarily" of nonviolent tactics. This monograph thus conceptualizes campaigns along a continuum, from campaigns of almost perfect nonviolent discipline to armed insurgencies, as illustrated in Figure 1.[10]

Figure 1. *Nonviolent Discipline Spectrum*

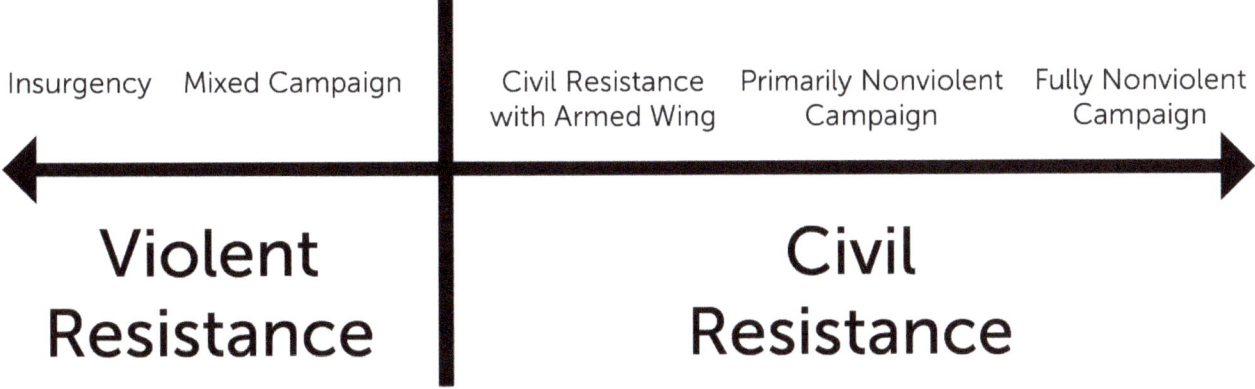

---

[9] Throughout the monograph, the terms "nonviolent methods" and "nonviolent tactics" are used interchangeably to refer to particular individual nonviolent actions, or, as Ackerman and Kruegler define them: "behavior toward the opponents and their agents in specific encounters" (Ackerman and Kruegler 1993, 7). Sharp described these as the "weapons system" of civil resistance (Sharp 1973, 113), and categorized a set of 198 specific methods in three broad categories of "Protest and Persuasion," "Noncooperation," and "Nonviolent Intervention." While Sharp's classification is quite granular, other scholars describe tactics in broader terms such as "strike, boycotts, mass demonstrations...and the creation of alternative institutions" (Zunes et al 1999, 2).

[10] For a similar conceptualization, see Zunes 1994.

This definition is not intended to denigrate the value of other, more theoretical definitions of violence and nonviolent discipline. Critically, scholars and philosophers have expanded our conception of violence to more subtle and indirect forms of oppression such as structural violence or culturally entrenched discrimination. However, this monograph maintains that it is useful on its own merits to understand when civil resistance campaigns will suffer from breakdowns in nonviolent discipline defined in this narrower and more empirical way.

Sources of Nonviolent Discipline: Ethical and Strategic

Since the topic of nonviolent discipline has been relatively under-researched to date, there are few major debates between scholars around this issue. Perhaps the most salient related debate is the question of whether civil resistance should be primarily "principled" or "pragmatic."[11] The first suggests that nonviolent discipline should be derived from a belief or conviction, while the second suggests that nonviolent discipline is derived from strategic considerations (Boserup and Mack 1974, Burrowes 1996, May 2015, Nepstad 2015, Schock 2015). This relates to the question of the very definition of "nonviolence" or "nonviolent action" referenced above, as several authors argue that to truly be nonviolent action, civil resistance must incorporate moral elements (Randle 1994, Burrowes 1996).

The influential figures of Mahatma Gandhi and Gene Sharp are typically referred to as inspirations in this debate. Those who draw more on Gandhi see nonviolent action as an inescapably moral practice while those following Sharp view it more as a pragmatic means of achieving political change (Schock 2005). Neither of these authors can be considered fully "principled" or "pragmatic." Both emphasize the intermingling of principled and pragmatic factors. However, Gandhi emphasizes that nonviolent force is not just a method of political struggle but also, critically, a matter of spiritual practice and discovery of the truth (Gandhi 1999). This has made his work a central inspiration for those who approach nonviolent action from a more "principled" perspective. Conversely, Sharp's work emphasizes that nonviolent action is an effective method of achieving political change that does not necessarily require any kind of moral or ethical

---

[11] See, for example: Clements 2015 and Howes 2013.

commitment (Sharp 1973, 1979, 2005). This has made him a seminal source for those approaching nonviolent action from a more "pragmatic" perspective.

In actual civil resistance struggles there are no sharp dividing lines between the pragmatic and the principled. In fact, few major civil resistance campaigns have been led by pacifists. As George Lakey says: "Most pacifists do not practice nonviolent resistance and most people who do practice nonviolent resistance are not pacifists" (Lakey 1987, 87). Ackerman and Kruegler go so far as to argue that "In the overwhelming majority of known cases of nonviolent conflict, there is no evidence that concepts of principled nonviolence were either present or contributed in a significant way to the outcome" (Ackerman and Kruegler 1993, 4).

Yet many ostensibly "pragmatic" civil resistance campaigns have drawn on "principled" ideas to strengthen their nonviolent character (Sorensen and Vinthagen 2012), and many movements consider the choice of nonviolent action to be inescapably both principled and pragmatic, based on the insight that the means of political struggle often prefigure its ends (Randle 1994). Principles and pragmatism are often entwined and overlapping categories.

> *In actual civil resistance struggles there are no sharp dividing lines between the pragmatic and the principled.*

The two orientations provide different interpretations of the significance of nonviolent discipline: For the first, breakdowns in nonviolent discipline are moral failures which undermine the movement's identity. For the second, breakdowns in nonviolent discipline are strategic failures, regrettable primarily because they undermine the political dynamics of effective civil resistance, such as alienating potential domestic allies or third-party supporters (Sharp 2005, 489) and legitimizing violent repression (Binnendijk and Marovic 2006).

Empirically, the two approaches imply fairly similar patterns of behavior regarding nonviolent discipline: In both cases campaign leadership should discourage their followers from engaging in violence. However, while this general pattern should hold broadly for the campaign leaders motivated by principles of pacifism, leaders motivated more by pragmatism and strategic considerations may or may not tolerate breaches in nonviolent discipline depending on their views of what enhances overall effectiveness of the struggle. This question will be considered at greater length in the empirical discussion which follows.

Leaders of particular civil resistance campaigns have offered extensive suggestions for encouraging or maintaining nonviolent discipline. One particularly vibrant example is the Nashville Schools organized by James Lawson during the Civil Rights Movement that taught principles of nonviolent action and trained participants in maintaining nonviolent discipline through role-play and other exercises (Isaac et al 2012).

Other Sources of Nonviolent Discipline

Beyond the principled/pragmatic debate, various scholars who have compared civil resistance campaigns globally largely provide *ad hoc* suggestions for maintaining nonviolent discipline. Sharp (1973) offers at least 18 suggestions for movements to encourage nonviolent discipline, such as sending marshals to organize demonstrations, keeping physical space between protesters and opponents, and requiring participants to sign codes of conduct. While his suggestions are rich and complex they are presented with little reference as to which of the recommendations are appropriate at particular times or what the relationship between particular suggestions is. For example, Sharp calls on civil resistance leaders both to call off the campaign if they fear breakdowns in nonviolent discipline and to organize more nonviolent actions as a way of re-directing anger and other emotions which might lead to violence. Yet he does not offer a consistent theory for when either of these opposing suggestions will be called for.

Several authors describe the importance of training for confrontation as a factor in promoting nonviolent discipline. Richard Gregg suggested that effective training for nonviolent resistance could be a process as long, or longer, than the training process for becoming a soldier (Gregg 1935). Stephan says that nonviolent discipline comes from leadership, training and communication (Stephan 2006). Nepstad also points to the importance of training and preparation, as well as appeals from leaders for participants to remain nonviolent, and points in particular to the influence religious figures can have in improving nonviolent discipline (Nepstad 2011). Training in resisting the impulse to respond to violence with violence was a central part of Gandhi's campaign for Indian independence, and was powerfully integrated into major aspects of the US Civil Rights Campaign by transformational leaders such as Martin Luther King, Jr., James Lawson and others (Ackerman and DuVall 2000, Isaac et al 2012).

Selective participation is also a factor considered important by many in maintaining nonviolent discipline. Prior training in nonviolent discipline for campaign activists may not be effective if campaign events are also attended by "outsiders" who are not invested in the campaign's commitment to nonviolent discipline. Thus, Sharp (1973, 2005) suggests a system of membership restrictions, keeping out potential participants not committed to nonviolent action. Mattaini (2013) and Helvey (2004) both discuss this question in regard to youth participation. While young people bring energy to a campaign they may "exhibit thuggish characteristics" (Helvey 2004, 15) if not carefully trained and organized.

Various aspects of campaign leadership and structure may also affect nonviolent discipline. Mattaini suggests that campaign organizers' openness to the ideas and strategies of their followers is likely to encourage nonviolent discipline, with participants less likely to "break the rules" if they are given input on how and when the rules are implemented (Mattaini 2013, 100). He argues that a more open, participatory structure which encourages debate and dissent will encourage nonviolent discipline.

In contrast, several authors argue that campaign cohesion, that is, whether the campaign as a whole sticks together in a single organization or fragments into many competing organizations, and the presence of a centralized hierarchical leadership structure are important for promoting nonviolent discipline. The most extensive examination of this question comes from political scientist Wendy Pearlman (2011). Pearlman argues that cohesion is necessary for nonviolent civil resistance because maintaining nonviolent discipline requires coordination and collective restraint, which are only possible in a cohesive campaign. Campaign fragmentation, on the other hand, encourages violence as splinter groups "outbid" each other for recruits and attention by engaging in more and more extreme and confrontational tactics.

While these generalized arguments about factors that increase nonviolent discipline have been crucial in advancing our understanding, what is lacking in the literature to date is a systematic theory connecting the various approaches. It is also lacking comprehensive testing of how well the various factors perform when measured against one another. The following section provides a unifying framework through the use of a simple mathematical model, while the sections thereafter provide some initial testing of a variety of expected influences on nonviolent discipline presented in the literature or implied by the model.

A Theory of Nonviolent Discipline

This section builds a theory of nonviolent discipline around the decision of a campaign participant to engage in violent or nonviolent action. The approach can be roughly described as "rational choice" but utilizes a very "thin" definition of rationality which simply assumes that individuals operate on the basis of a certain set of preferences and are sensitive to the possibilities of reward or punishment.[12]

The theory is structured using the logical device of a formal mathematical model. This formal model provides a few key advantages for examining the question of nonviolent discipline. First, it provides a simple and logically clear framework in which to consider the question. Second, it provides a way to incorporate the various explanations of nonviolent discipline from the pre-existing literature into a single unified explanation. Third, it suggests an additional set of expected influences on nonviolent discipline.

Consider an individual participating in an anti-government demonstration in a non-democracy. Assume also that the demonstration organizers have called on their participants to remain nonviolent. What will motivate the individual to follow this call?

First, every individual has a certain set of prior preferences for violent or nonviolent resistance. More static factors such as personal inclinations or aversion towards violence, or cultural norms, play a big part in shaping these preferences. However, more immediate factors such as previous training in civil resistance or in armed combat may also affect them over the short term. Let b_v represent the individual's preference for violent action, and b_{nv} represent their preference for nonviolent action.[13]

Second, the individual must take into account the potential consequences of her action. While the individual may prefer one form of resistance, she may alter her choice if her preferred choice will result in significant personal costs. In this regard two key actors bear consideration: the regime and the nonviolent campaign. How will both of these actors respond to the individual's choice?

Regimes often seek to repress any form of political dissent (Davenport 2007). Yet in many cases the intensity and regularity of this repression varies depending on whether the dissent is violent or nonviolent (Lichbach 1987). For instance, the regime may choose to repress violent resistance more strongly than nonviolent resistance because it perceives violence as more directly threatening its power, or because the repression of violent resistance will not lead to external condemnation (Sharp 1973). Let r represent

---

[12] For an explanation of this broad approach to rational choice, see Riker 1995.

[13] Manipulating these internal preferences is a major focus of many works on civil resistance motivated more by ethical principles. Richard Gregg, for example, extensively discusses the "development of sentiments appropriate to non-violence" and argues that "if a non-violent resister has not thoroughly cultivated the requisite sentiments he will, by inevitable working of psychological law, fail in a prolonged intense struggle." Gregg 1935, 191.

Chapter 1: Literature Review and Theory

the intensity of expected repression, with r_v the intensity of regime repression against violent action and r_{nv} the expected intensity of regime repression against nonviolent action. The individual considers repression likely to occur with probability p_v for violent action and p_{nv} for nonviolent action.

Finally, the nonviolent campaign may itself reward or punish the activist for her choice. Based on our assumption that the activist is a member of a civil resistance campaign, it follows that the campaign will have an interest in keeping its followers nonviolent, and thus may develop some mechanism of rewarding or punishing people for this behavior.

The spectrum of rewards or punishments is extremely broad and does not necessarily involve either monetary or physical reward or punishment. Rewards can be as simple as positive affirmation from peers or being praised by movement leaders. Punishments can be as abstract as the pangs of conscience from disappointing a respected leader or violating a personal commitment. Let s_v represent the intensity of expected reward or punishment for violent action, and s_{nv} the intensity of anticipated reward or punishment for nonviolent action. As with repression, the individual also considers this reward or punishment as being likely with certain probabilities p_v and p_{nv}.

The individual's decision of resistance method can thus be modeled in a simple way through the following equation. The individual will choose nonviolent resistance, and thus maintain nonviolent discipline, under the following conditions:

$$b_{nv} - p_{nv}(r_{nv}) + p_{nv}(s_{nv}) > b_v - p_v(r_v) + p_v(s_v)$$

Table 1. *Mathematical Model Elements*

b_{nv}	Personal benefit/preference for nonviolent action.
r_{nv}	Expected intensity of repression from the government for nonviolent action.
s_{nv}	Expected intensity of punishment/reward from campaign for nonviolent action.
p_{nv}	Probability of a particular response to nonviolent action (used for both government repression and campaign punishment/reward).
b_v	Personal benefit/preference for violent action.
r_v	Expected intensity of repression from the government for violent action.
s_v	Expected intensity of punishment/reward from campaign for violent action.
p_v	Probability of a particular response to violent action (used for both government repression and campaign punishment/reward).

In simple terms, the proposed theory argues that an individual will choose nonviolent action over violent action when her personal preference for nonviolent action, minus the expected intensity of repression for nonviolent action and plus the expected reward of nonviolent action, is greater than the personal preference for violent action, minus the expected intensity of repression for violent action and plus the expected reward of violent action.

This mathematical modeling is useful for two reasons: First, it gives a sense of how various strategies to maintain nonviolent discipline might relate to one another. Instead of looking at factors such as government repression or campaign means of rewarding participants in isolation, it provides a framework for thinking about how all these various factors interrelate in motivating the individual activist's choice of tactics.

Second, it provides a framework to consider systematically what factors will be important in generating and sustaining nonviolent discipline. The framework is intentionally abstract, yet it provides several points of entry for the academic and the practitioner. Nonviolent discipline can be encouraged through manipulating each of the eight factors presented above (and listed in Table 1). Each of these factors is open to adjustments in intensity or level if treated by an outside stimulus from the campaign peers or leadership.

For example, civil resistance campaigns can seek to increase nonviolent discipline through increasing b_{nv} through communication about civil resistance's effectiveness and ethical or ideological arguments about the superiority of nonviolent resistance to violent resistance. Campaigns can also seek to reduce either the probability or the intensity of repression of nonviolent resistance through mixing confrontational tactics such as sit-ins with less confrontational tactics such as stay-away strikes or boycotts (Schock 2005), or through canceling actions in which repression is expected. And finally, perhaps the factors most amenable to campaign manipulation are the probability and intensity of reward for nonviolent behavior and punishment for violent behavior.

Expected Influences on Nonviolent Discipline

The monograph now proposes a series of factors expected to increase nonviolent discipline. This list of factors blends the *ad hoc* recommendations from the earlier literature with the simple theory of nonviolent discipline in civil resistance described above.

Chapter 1: Literature Review and Theory

First, a country's historical experience of nonviolent and violent resistance is likely to strongly affect nonviolent discipline. Historical experience runs through several of the factors in the mathematical model, from the personal preference factors b_{nv} and b_v to expectations of the likelihood and severity of repression (r_v and r_{nv}) and campaign punishments and rewards (s_v and s_{nv}). If the country has a long tradition of successful nonviolent contention, the individual is likely to perceive greater value in participation in nonviolent action. Similarly, if there is a historical tradition of successful violent struggle, the individual is likely to put a lower value on maintaining nonviolent discipline.

Yet historical experience does not translate immediately to individuals. While major nonviolent and violent campaigns may become important historical milestones, their memory can fade over time or be erased through censorship or the valorization of violence. For example, the successful independence struggles of many post-colonial countries involved major movements of civil resistance, yet their nonviolent collective characters are often left out of historical textbooks and must be "recovered" by later scholars (Bartkowski 2013).

This process of knowledge transmission need not be limited to a country's own history. Knowledge of civil resistance struggles in other nations and the dynamics of civil resistance may also increase nonviolent discipline. This may be particularly the case when countries are in close geographical proximity to or share common cultural norms with other countries with successful histories of civil resistance, facilitating a process of norm and tactical diffusion (Bunce and Wolchik 2011, Gleditsch and Rivera 2015, Braithwaite et al 2015). Yet diffusion is not a simple physical process. For knowledge of the history and dynamics of civil resistance to reach cohering movements or potential campaign participants, they need to receive some form of training, education or lateral technical assistance from seasoned practitioners (Isaac et al 2012). Thus, in regard to the historical experience of struggle, there are two key interacting factors which may affect nonviolent discipline that are articulated in the following expected influences on nonviolent discipline.

> **Influence 1:** Nonviolent discipline will be higher in countries with experiences of successful civil resistance and lower in countries with experiences of failed civil resistance. Nonviolent discipline will be lower in countries with experiences of successful violent resistance and higher in countries with experiences of failed violent resistance.

Influence 2: Nonviolent discipline will be higher in campaigns with widespread knowledge of past civil resistance campaigns, particularly when spread through formal training.

Related to the historical experience of civil resistance is the existence of a wide range of knowledge sources on civil resistance strategies and tactics.[14] Social movement scholars have observed that individuals and groups seeking to pursue a political goal tend to reproduce the strategies and tactics that have been used historically in similar political struggles in their country. For example, activists in the "Black Lives Matter" movement have drawn inspiration not solely from the ideas but also from particular methods used in the Civil Rights Movement of the 1960s.[15] While major tactical innovations do sometimes occur in particular movements, this innovation typically happens only incrementally and at the margins (Tarrow 1993).

The wider and more diverse the set of civil resistance strategies and tactics that have been used in a country in the past, the more likely individuals will have personal experience with or knowledge about nonviolent methods that they can draw on in situations of conflict. This relates less to tactics which are considered historically efficacious, as stipulated in the first influence identified above, and more to those tactics which are cognitively available based on past experience. For example, Smithey (2013) points to several ways in which past participation in civil resistance actions can shape individuals' collective identity, making them more likely to continue civil resistance in the future. In terms of the theory, the existence of wide, diverse tactical choices affects individuals' internal preferences for nonviolent action and decreases their preferences for violent action (increasing b_{nv} and decreasing b_v) Succinctly, the expected influence may be stated as follows:

Influence 3: Nonviolent discipline will be higher in countries that saw the use of a wide range of diverse nonviolent tactics in the past.

Another important influence is the opportunities present in the external political environment.[16] In a contemporary political environment that rewards nonviolent action with political concessions, it is more likely that movement participants will find greater

---

[14] In the social mobilization literature this is typically called a country's "repertoire of contention." See Tilly 2010 and Tarrow 1998.
[15] See for instance: Day 2015 or Canon and Schatz 2015.
[16] In the academic literature, this is typically referred to as the "political opportunity structure." See, for example: Kitschelt 1986.

value in maintaining nonviolent discipline. This should increase the personal value assigned to nonviolent behavior (the b_{nv} factor), thus encouraging nonviolent discipline.

Influence 4: Nonviolent discipline will be higher the more frequently civil resistance wins political concessions.

There are several characteristics of the civil resistance campaign itself that may affect levels of nonviolent discipline. First, strong, consistent messages from campaign organizers that encourage resistance to be solely nonviolent are likely to encourage nonviolent discipline. This relationship relates to both the probability (p_{nv}) and intensity (s_{nv}) of campaign punishment for violent action. Consistent appeals for nonviolent discipline make it clear that such behavior is unacceptable to the campaign. If movement leaders are unclear regarding the importance of nonviolent behavior, then individual participants should expect that punishment for violations of nonviolent discipline is less likely, and if it occurs will likely be less severe. As these expectations change, nonviolent discipline in all probability will become more fragile.

This expected influence speaks to the debate over whether civil resistance should be motivated by "principled" appeals to ethical principles or "pragmatic" appeals to the tactical superiority of nonviolent action. While both may offer messages calling for nonviolent discipline, one would expect those motivated by pacifism to be more consistent. Campaign leaders motivated solely by pragmatism may change their message based on what they perceive to be "pragmatic" actions at a given point in struggle.[17] Campaign participants may also interpret their appeals to pragmatism or need for a strategic efficacy in their own terms, implying that nonviolent discipline may not be an absolute value if they no longer believe it to be effective.

This is by no means fully determinative. Appeals for nonviolent discipline on strategic or pragmatic grounds can certainly unequivocally call for nonviolent discipline, for instance by calling for consistency between means and ends in order for nonviolent action to lead to more peaceful political change and a less violent society. However, if appeals for nonviolent discipline are made on the grounds of absolute moral or ethical principles, it is even less likely that participants might believe that a violation of nonviolent

---

[17] Such shifts would, of course, go against the theory of civil resistance advocated for by civil resistance scholars, which points to any breakdown in nonviolent discipline as undermining the fundamental mechanisms of nonviolent action (Sharp 1973, Ackerman and Kruegler 1993). However, they are all too common among "on the ground" leaders of civil resistance campaigns. This phenomenon is discussed in more depth in the case study section.

discipline would be acceptable.

Influence 5: Clear messaging from movement leaders which consistently demands nonviolent discipline will increase nonviolent discipline.

Even if certain leaders consistently call for nonviolent discipline, if the campaign leadership itself is fragmented and weak this should similarly reduce the expected likelihood and intensity of campaign punishment to discipline its members. Clear, hierarchical campaign leadership with a recognized authority to discipline its members would be one key way of ensuring that the campaign is able to enforce nonviolent discipline.

In addition, if campaign leaders are internally divided, campaign participants may perceive them as less capable of monitoring individual behavior and punishing violations of nonviolent discipline. This division would be most prominently displayed in campaign internal conflicts, in which leaders visibly fight over policies, strategies or control over campaign resources. As the level of internal conflict and division within the campaign rises, its ability to punish individual violations of nonviolent discipline would be severely hampered. In contrast, campaign participants are likely to perceive campaign leadership with strong bases of authority and unity rather than division as more effective in monitoring and punishing potential violations of nonviolent discipline.

Influence 6: Strong, cohesive campaign leadership will increase nonviolent discipline.[18]

The goals that campaigns articulate may also shape the individual's judgment of the appropriateness and desirability of violent vs. nonviolent resistance. In situations where campaigns frame their goals as particularly revolutionary, such as the immediate departure of a particular ruler, individual participants may perceive a need to adopt similarly "extreme" tactics of violent resistance. If a campaign articulates more reformist goals which fit within current political discourse, then violent action may be perceived as inappropriate, and individual participants may be more likely to limit their behavior to nonviolent action.

---

[18] This expected influence draws on Wendy Pearlman's research on the Palestinian national movement (mentioned above) but also expands it to take into account the individual motives argued for in the monograph's theory of nonviolent discipline.

Chapter 1: Literature Review and Theory

Influence 7: Nonviolent discipline will be higher in campaigns which articulate moderate or reformist goals.

The immediate physical situation can also critically shape individual decisions. In situations of extreme confrontation individuals may experience feelings of anger or threat or a desire to not back down, making them more likely to engage in violent behavior. Campaign leaders can influence these emotions by making tactical choices that involve low levels of confrontation and move from physically confrontational tactics to less confrontational tactics. For example, organizers might abandon tactics that place civil resisters in close proximity to the adversary's police forces such as street demonstrations, in favor of less confrontational tactics such as strikes, boycotts or cultural acts of resistance (e.g. humor, satire, resistance music) when threatened with repression.[19]

In contrast, we would expect tactics that rely heavily on direct physical confrontations to make breakdowns in nonviolent discipline more likely. With nonviolent methods such as sit-ins or nonviolent blockades, the confrontational physical positioning of campaign participants may lead to a highly-charged emotional atmosphere in which violence becomes more appealing.

Influence 8: Nonviolent discipline will be higher in campaigns that make tactical choices to avoid direct physical confrontation.

All of the characteristics of the national experience and the civil resistance campaign described above will likely have an effect on the distribution of individual attitudes towards violent and nonviolent resistance. In some countries with long histories of successful civil resistance and many diverse nonviolent tactical choices available, where civil resistance campaigns are led by leaders clearly calling for nonviolent discipline, the opportunities for violent action may be extremely limited.

However, some potential civil resistance campaign participants may simply be inclined towards violent action due to personal histories or a genetic propensity for violence (McDermott et al 2013). Furthermore, certain populations, such as young unmarried men, may be particularly prone to engage in violent behavior (Helvey 2004,

---

[19] It bears mentioning that methods of noncooperation may certainly be perceived as confrontational, and still impose significant costs on the opponent. The point here is that a less physically confrontational tactic removes the individual campaign participant from a high-pressure situation in which hot emotions may influence them to break nonviolent discipline.

Mattaini 2013). In terms of the presented theory of nonviolent discipline, some people may have such a high level of internal preference for violent action (a high b_v factor) that no outside influence matters. Considering this in terms of campaign strategy, because some people may be almost inevitably drawn to violent action, campaigns can improve nonviolent discipline through a system of membership criteria that excludes those judged likely to engage in violence.[20]

> **Influence 9:** Nonviolent discipline will be higher in campaigns which have some system of membership criteria that exclude those likely to engage in violence.

However, while we might intuitively expect limiting participation to those committed to nonviolent action to increase nonviolent discipline, broad, diverse participation itself may also increase nonviolent discipline. If participation is limited to a particular subset of society, activists may fall prey to dynamics of "othering" or dehumanization, lowering social stigmas for engaging in violence and increasing the b_v (internal preference for violence) factor. In contrast, if campaigns have broad, diverse participation from all sectors of society, including members of the "oppressing" group this may lower the likelihood of "othering" and thus reduce the appeal of participating in violence towards campaign opponents.

This argument is the inverse of arguments from Chenoweth and Stephan (2011) on how broad, diverse participation may reduce repression. Chenoweth and Stephan argue that security forces are less likely to repress protesters when they have personal connections to the campaign. For example, police facing protesters in Serbia's "Bulldozer Revolution" of 2000 reported that they refused to follow orders to fire on the protesters because they knew their children were among them (Chenoweth and Stephan 2011, 47). In the same way, campaign participants may be less likely to engage in violent resistance if the people in the campaign have personal connections to the people in the government and security forces. Having a campaign with extremely broad, diverse participation increases the likelihood that such connections between the campaign and the opponent will occur.

Diversity might also encourage nonviolent discipline through presenting a picture

---

[20] For an in-depth examination of such a system of membership requirements at work, see Masullo J. 2015 on the Peace Community of San José de Apartadó in Colombia.

of society as a whole engaging in resistance. Peaceful civil resistance actions may be able to attract large sections of society who would be unwilling or unable to participate in violence, such as the disabled, the children or the elderly. The picture of such diverse participation alone may serve as a powerful reminder to those inclined to violence of the potential power of nonviolent action, increasing their preference for it (the b_{nv} factor), and decreasing the likelihood of breakdowns in nonviolent discipline.

Influence 10: Nonviolent discipline will be higher in campaigns with high levels of diversity.

Even if campaigns offer consistent messaging supporting nonviolent resistance and have cohesive leadership to offer this message clearly and consistently, individuals with a high preference for violent resistance (b_v) and low preference for nonviolent resistance (b_{nv}) may still be motivated to engage in violent resistance. Campaigns can avert this by increasing the reward for remaining nonviolent or increasing punishments for engaging in violence. Following the logic of the theory laid out above, the insight here is that even individuals who have a strong preference for violent action (b_v) may choose nonviolent action instead if the punishments for violence will be sufficiently severe.

These punishments, as mentioned above, need not be direct or physical. For example, the fear of social ostracism or isolation can be a powerful motivator. Other mechanisms proposed in the literature, such as signing a code of conduct before participating in the campaign (Mattaini 2013), can also be a way of imposing punishments, as individuals may feel guilt over breaking their word even if no *post facto* physical punishment occurs.

Influence 11: Nonviolent discipline will be higher when individuals receive some form of personal punishment from the campaign for engaging in violent resistance.

Patterns of state repression are also likely to have a strong impact on patterns of nonviolent discipline (Lichbach 1987, Moore 1998). The theory laid out above points us to look at the question of repression in a slightly more complex fashion than simply arguing that nonviolent discipline is less likely in repressive environments. Instead, examining the question in terms of a choice between violent action and nonviolent action directs us to consider the relative intensity and likelihood of repression for different tactics of either violent or nonviolent resistance. Assuming that an individual has sufficient motivation to engage in dissent,[21] the question becomes what action is more likely to result in severe repression. Consistency of repression for particular tactics in the recent pact, violent or nonviolent, is thus key as it shapes the perceived likelihood of present-day repression (Cunningham and Beaulieu 2010). In simple terms the expected relationship between nonviolent discipline and repression is as follows:

> **Influence 12:** Nonviolent discipline will be higher as the frequency and intensity of government repression of violent resistance increase. Nonviolent discipline will be lower as the frequency and intensity of government repression of nonviolent resistance increase.

Finally, as campaigns develop over time, one might expect breakdowns in nonviolent discipline to become more common. If the campaign is unable to achieve its goal quickly, campaign participants may become disillusioned with civil resistance, reducing their preference for it (b_{nv}) and thus increasing their relative preference for violence. This change in preferences brought about through disillusionment may find expression in violent actions or allegiance to more radical ideologies. In the Civil Rights Movement, for instance, disillusionment over the pace of change after several years of nonviolent action helped fuel the rise of the Black Power movement and militant organizations such as the Black Panthers (Garrow 1986). More recently in Syria, when months of almost entirely peaceful nonviolent actions failed to oust President Bashar al-Assad, the anti-Assad opposition began to increasingly turn to violent resistance, helping to lead that country into civil war (Bartkowski and Taleb 2015).

> **Influence 13:** Nonviolent discipline will become progressively harder to maintain as a campaign continues over time.

All of these expected influences, as well as the methods of testing in the following sections, are summarized in Table 2 on the following page. This set of expected influences, while large, is not intended to be a comprehensive listing of the empirical implications of the theory of nonviolent discipline. Rather, they represent a first selection of arguments from the literature that can be integrated with the proposed theory. The

---

[21] This question of how to explain the choice of participation or non-participation is critical but has already been extensively studied in the literature on various forms of political dissent and is separate from the key question of this monograph. For classic works on the decision to engage in dissent see Tilly 1978, Lichbach 1995, or Wood 2003.

sections that follow test these relationships statistically and later qualitatively to begin to understand which of these influences most consistently affects nonviolent discipline.

Table 2. Expected Influences for Testing

	Factors Increasing Nonviolent Discipline	Testing Method
1	Historical Experience of Violent and Nonviolent Contention	Statistical/ Case Studies
2	Information and Training on Civil Resistance Campaigns	Case Studies Only
3	Wide Range of Civil Resistance Tactics	Statistical/ Case Studies
4	External Political Environment Rewarding Nonviolent Action	Statistical/ Case Studies
5	Appeals from Movement Leaders for Nonviolent Discipline	Case Studies Only
6	Strong, Cohesive Campaign Leadership	Statistical/ Case Studies
7	Moderate Strategic Goals	Statistical/ Case Studies
8	Tactical Choices to Avoid Confrontation	Statistical/ Case Studies
9	Membership Criteria Excluding Violent Actors	Statistical/ Case Studies
10	High Levels of Diversity	Statistical/ Case Studies
11	Campaign Punishments for Violent Actions	Case Studies Only
12	Discriminating Repression of Violent Resistance	Statistical/ Case Studies
13	Length of the Campaign	Statistical/ Case Studies

Chapter 2
Statistical Analysis and Results

This section presents the results of statistical tests of several of the expected influences on nonviolent discipline laid out above. For ease of reading, most of the technical information on the structure of the data, the methods of testing, and tests for statistical robustness have been included in a statistical annex (Appendix A). For academic readers interested in this aspect of the research, the annex is the more appropriate reading. For more general readers not as familiar with advanced statistics, this section will be more accessible.

As mentioned in the introduction, the data used for the testing come from the Nonviolent and Violent Campaigns and Outcomes (NAVCO) 3.0 data collection project (Chenoweth, Pinckney, and Lewis 2016). NAVCO 3.0 collects detailed information on individual tactical actions deployed, on the one hand, by anti-government campaigns, including demonstrations, strikes, boycotts and sit-ins by civil resistance campaigns, and on the other, terrorist attacks and armed clashes by violent insurgencies. This level of detail is important for examining questions of nonviolent discipline since it allows the observer to look at the unique characteristics of individual actions rather than looking broadly at the vaguer picture of campaigns as a whole.

Looking at more detailed data like this also allows us to examine how factors such as patterns of repression or concessions to nonviolent action change over time. For example, for each action by a civil resistance campaign, the data are able to capture how many other nonviolent and violent actions in the country in the recent past were repressed or received concessions. This gives a fine-grained view of what the political opportunities and challenges of repression look like at each individual moment of a civil resistance campaign. The statistical tests thus collect information on the average number of nonviolent actions in the recent past that were repressed, as well as those receiving some form of concessions from the government.[22]

---

[22] These patterns are averaged over different numbers of past actions. The primary testing variable is the average number of actions repressed or gaining concessions over the last 25 nonviolent actions. For more detail, see the statistical annex.

This relationship is illustrated in Figure 2 below, in which information on repression patterns over five most recent nonviolent actions is used to generate an "average repression" score for a particular action. The five most recent nonviolent actions were repressed three out of five times, giving the current nonviolent action (labeled "NV Action 6" in the figure) a "past repression score" of 60%. Influence 12, described above, suggests that as this score increases the likelihood of nonviolent discipline being maintained during NV Action 6 will decrease.

Figure 2. *Illustrating Past Repression Influence*

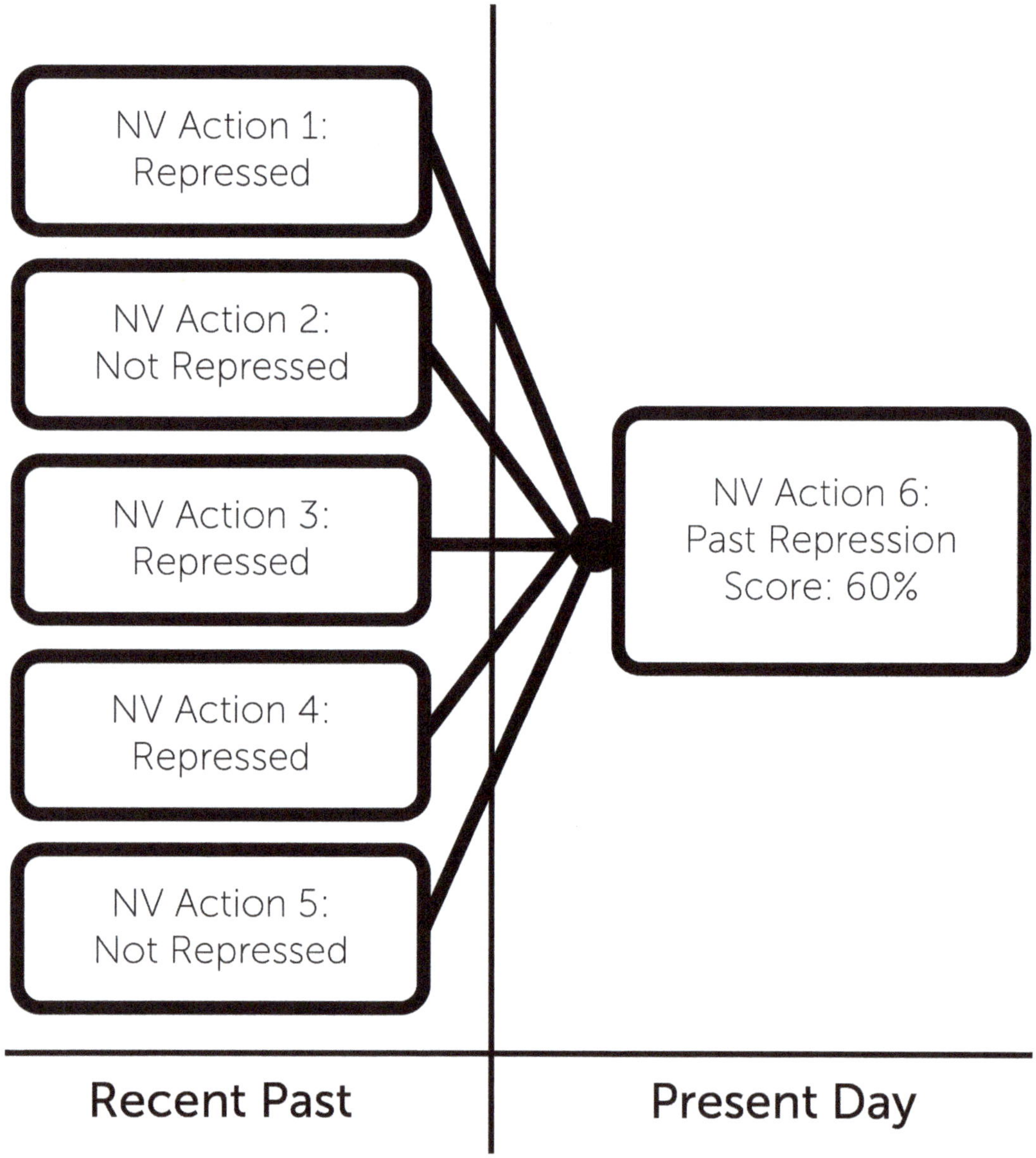

Chapter 2: Statistical Analysis and Results

The data used in this study cover thousands of actions by hundreds of campaigns in 14 countries from the years 1991 through 2012.[23] While some of the countries were democratic for part of this time period, the study only looks at actions by campaigns during periods of non-democratic rule.

The statistical tests sought to determine which characteristics of the country, the campaign, or the individual action follow the expected influences identified and described in the previous section and made it more likely that a particular action would be nonviolent, violent, or "mixed" between violent and nonviolent elements.[24] Details of how these measures were developed are included in the statistical annex. For the list of expected relationships that were tested statistically, refer to Figure 2 on the preceding page.

Results of the Statistical Tests

Initial analysis of the data revealed that violent and nonviolent action follow many of the expected patterns articulated in the literature. For example, violent actions by civil resistance campaigns are much more likely to face repression than nonviolent actions. Governments repressed violent or "mixed" events almost 70% of the time while only repressing nonviolent events 12% of the time.

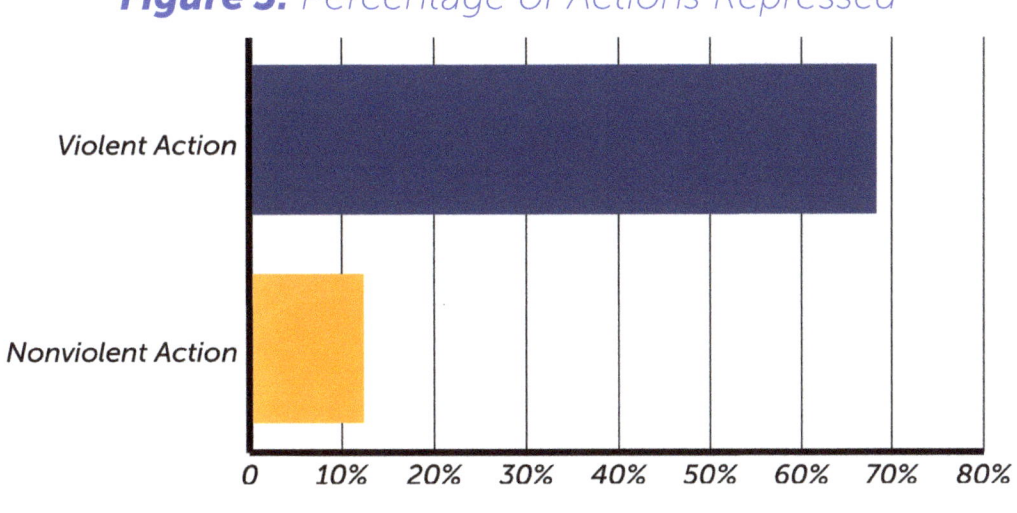

Figure 3. *Percentage of Actions Repressed*

---

[23] The countries are Algeria, Bahrain, Egypt, Kenya, Libya, Madagascar, Mexico, Morocco, Pakistan, Sudan, Tunisia, Ukraine, Uzbekistan and Yemen.
[24] For example, a largely nonviolent demonstration in which some participants engage in clashes with police would be a "mixed" action.

For violent and nonviolent action, concessions by the state opponent were rare. However, the state was much more likely to offer concessions in response to nonviolent action. The state gave concessions in response to nonviolent actions 2.5% of the time. In contrast, the state only gave concessions in response to violent and mixed actions 0.5% of the time.

How do these patterns of repression and concessions relate to the question of nonviolent discipline? There is one largely expected relationship and one surprising relationship. As expected, the most consistent predictor of breakdowns in nonviolent discipline by civil resistance campaigns is increasing levels of repression against nonviolent actions. As the number of nonviolent actions that were repressed by the government in the recent past increased, the likelihood of a breakdown in nonviolent discipline increased. On average across campaigns, moving from no repression over the last several nonviolent actions in the country to repression of all recent actions decreases the likelihood of maintaining nonviolent discipline by 19% when all other influences are kept constant.[25] This relationship closely follows the expectation laid out by the theory. As the costs of nonviolent action due to repression increase, individuals are less likely to perceive a benefit from remaining nonviolent and may choose violent action instead.

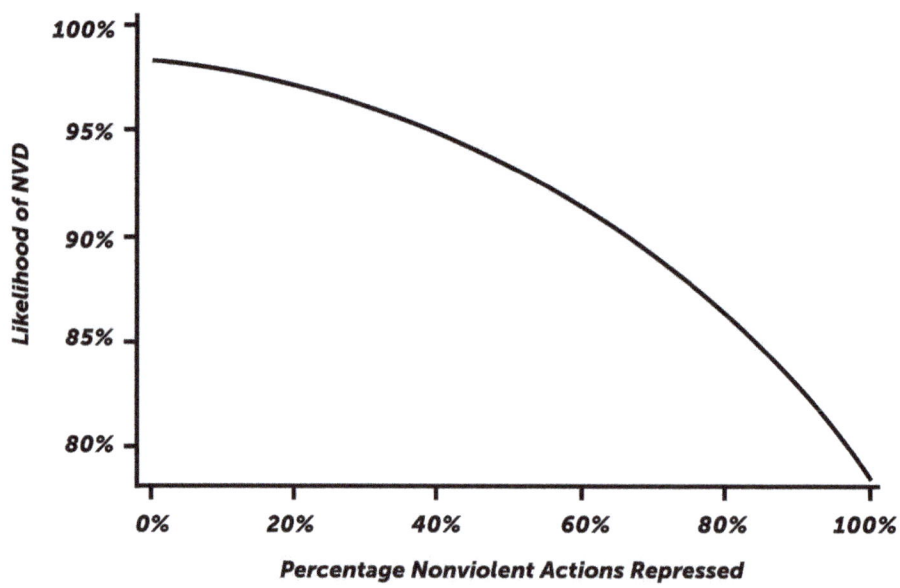

Figure 4. *Effects of Repression on Nonviolent Discipline*

---

[25] See the statistical annex for more information on how these predicted probabilities were derived. The primary statistical tests used a measure of the percentage of the last 25 nonviolent actions repressed.

Chapter 2: Statistical Analysis and Results

Figure 4 (on the preceding page) depicts this relationship graphically. As the percentage of nonviolent actions repressed in the recent past increases, the predicted likelihood of an action remaining nonviolent decreases, from a high of around a 98% predicted likelihood of nonviolent action to a 79% predicted likelihood of nonviolent action.

Patterns in the data suggest that this relationship is due more to campaign participants reacting to long-term patterns of repression rather than reacting immediately to regime repression with violence. Measures of average repression over the last 10 nonviolent actions or more all follow the same relationship, reducing the likelihood of a particular action being nonviolent in a statistically significant way. However, the same is not true of immediate repression. Whether the single nonviolent action immediately prior to a particular act was repressed does not have a significant impact on whether the act will be nonviolent. In other words, campaign participants do not immediately respond to repression with violent action. Instead, as the level of repression over the long term increases, participants become more and more likely to choose violence.

Surprisingly, the relationship is the same for concessions. The regime's dispensations toward the campaign do not strengthen nonviolent discipline as expected. Instead of concessions to past nonviolent action leading to increased nonviolent discipline, concessions seem to lead to a higher likelihood of breakdown in nonviolent discipline. A move from no concessions over the last 25 nonviolent actions to the maximum observed percentage of concessions decreases the likelihood of maintaining nonviolent discipline by almost 40%.[26]

The data are too broad to offer specific suggestions why this might be the case. However, various mechanisms are possible. The first is that concessions may lead campaigns to "rest on their laurels," in other words, achieving some concessions may make campaign leaders overconfident, causing them to lose focus. When they achieve some strategic progress, campaign leadership may relax the intensity of their training, their system of membership criteria, or other strict measures to maintain nonviolent discipline. Concessions from official channels may also inhibit the feeling of outrage over injustice that often unifies movements, leading to division and a breakdown in discipline (Martin 2007, 3).[27] Evidence from self-determination disputes suggests that

---

[26] Refer to Figure 2 and the discussion in the statistical annex for more information.
[27] Thanks to Brian Martin for suggesting this potential mechanism.

accommodation may also lead to increased splits in movements, with more radical groups dividing from moderates and pursuing more radical goals and violent methods (Cunningham 2013, 2014).

The effects of historical experience are as expected, but have inconsistent statistical significance. In the whole population of campaigns, they are not statistically significant. However, when only looking at major campaigns seeking regime change or secession the experiences of history do have their expected effects on nonviolent discipline, with past successful nonviolent campaigns associated with higher nonviolent discipline and past successful violent campaigns associated with lower nonviolent discipline.[28]

Several campaign characteristics are less significant for nonviolent discipline. Diversity in particular appears to have little or no relationship with nonviolent discipline. And the test of campaign criteria related to youth and students was similarly unclear, with inconsistent statistical results. Surprisingly, campaigns with hierarchical leadership and low levels of internal conflict, that is, campaigns with few visible disagreements between leaders over policy or strategy are actually more likely to have breakdowns in nonviolent discipline, with hierarchy decreasing the likelihood of maintaining nonviolent discipline by 35% and an increase in a campaign's level of internal conflict increasing the likelihood of maintaining nonviolent discipline by 28%.

Figure 5. *Campaign Structure and Likelihood of Maintaining Nonviolent Discipline*

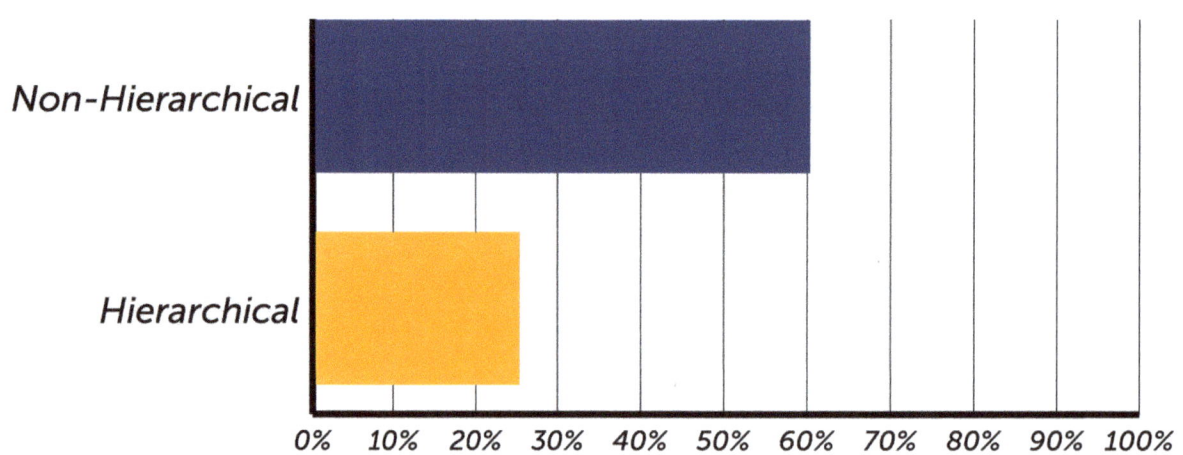

---

[28] Technically speaking, campaigns with revolutionary goals would include those against military occupations (Chenoweth and Stephan 2011); however the data used for this project contain no campaigns coded as anti-occupation.

Chapter 2: Statistical Analysis and Results

While these relationships are not predicted by the literature, one potential explanation for the finding about the negative impact of hierarchy on nonviolent discipline is that, following Mattaini rather than Pearlman, campaigns have greater nonviolent discipline when the actual participants have greater ownership over the actions taking place. Thus, in terms of the theory of nonviolent discipline, hierarchy may plausibly increase the likelihood, swiftness and intensity of punishment by campaign leadership of movement members breaking nonviolent discipline (the p_v and s_v factors in the mathematical model). However, it may also decrease the personal benefit an individual gains from staying nonviolent, as a participant might feel a lack of ownership for what is happening with the campaign she is part of (the b_{nv} factor). Alternately, anti-government movements may inherently attract rebellious recruits who may resist following hierarchical structures, leading to breakdowns in discipline.[29]

The internal conflict picture is also slightly more complicated when one digs deeper into the data. Almost all of the actions in the data take place in campaigns which either have no observed internal conflict or "cooperation with moderate disunity (i.e. ideological or policy disagreements)" (Chenoweth 2015). Thus the key difference that we observe in the statistical tests is that campaigns where there is some visible verbal disagreement have fewer breakdowns in nonviolent discipline. While visible verbal disagreements may indicate a problematic lack of campaign unity, they may also indicate that the campaign allows for a healthy degree of debate, thus increasing the feeling of a vested interest in the campaign itself among its participants. Multiple voices being heard may indicate that many different factions can claim ownership over the campaign and, being invested in its success, may be motivated to maintain stronger nonviolent discipline (increased b_{nv} factor). Campaigns which appear fully united at all times, on the other hand, may hide more covert internal disagreements rather than hash them out. If these disagreements do not come out in discussion within the campaign, they may be externalized in violent actions by campaign participants.

One other campaign characteristic which does appear to influence nonviolent discipline significantly is campaign goals. A revolutionary campaign goal of regime change or secession made maintaining nonviolent discipline 22% less likely. This change does not appear to be explained by differences in levels of repression. While

---

[29] Thanks to Erica Chenoweth for suggesting this.

actions by revolutionary campaigns are more likely to be repressed (29% of actions by revolutionary campaigns faced repression, compared with just 12% of actions by reformist campaigns), controlling for levels of repression does not eliminate the statistical significance of revolutionary goals in decreasing nonviolent discipline. Thus, while alternative explanations cannot be ruled out, it seems plausible that the reduced nonviolent discipline is related to revolutionary goals.

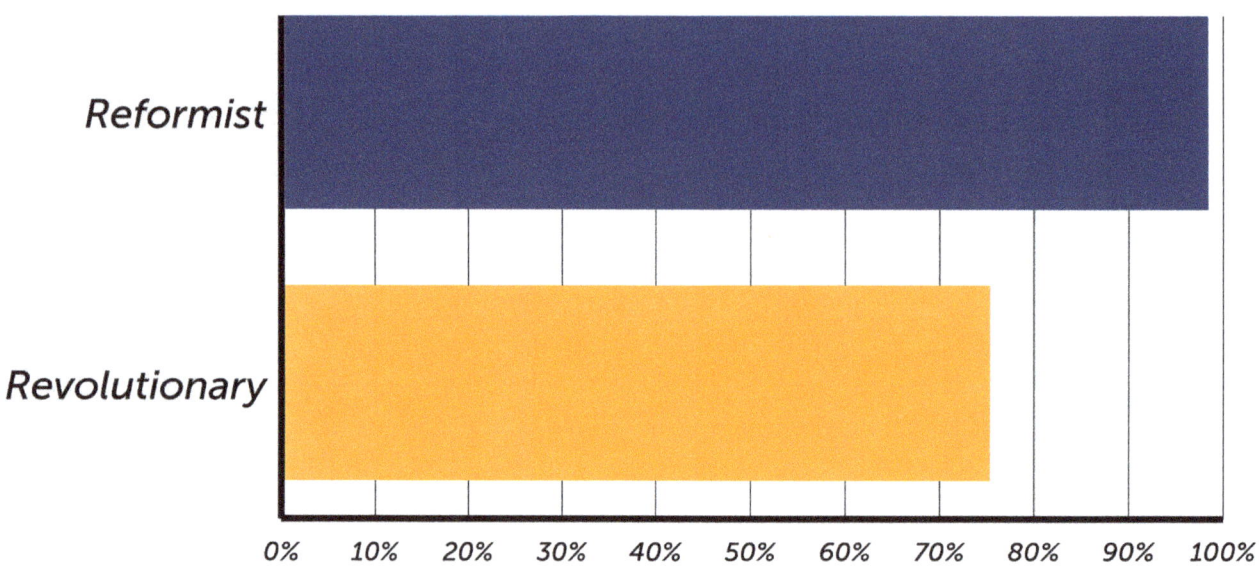

Figure 6. Strategic Goals and Likelihood of Maintaining Nonviolent Discipline

Finally, the duration of the campaign does appear to affect nonviolent discipline, though the effect is somewhat inconsistent. In most statistical tests, the length of time since the beginning of the campaign significantly predicted lower nonviolent discipline. In other words, as the campaign grew longer, actions were more and more likely to be violent. However, this relationship was not statistically significant across all tests, meaning that the influence of campaign length is inconsistent.

Statistical tests of whether physically confrontational tactics such as demonstrations or sit-ins led more frequently to breakdowns in nonviolent discipline were largely inconclusive. This was due in part to issues with the data (see the statistical annex for more information), but multiple tests do appear to be capturing genuine patterns in the data that show little or no relationship between specific tactics and the likelihood of maintaining nonviolent discipline. There are some minor indications that strikes may be

Chapter 2: Statistical Analysis and Results

slightly less prone to breakdowns in nonviolent discipline relative to protests or sit-ins, but this pattern is not statistically significant.

This finding supports the conclusions regarding the effects of repression, and more generally a picture of civil resistance campaign participants who respond to the incentives present in the broader political environment rather than simply reacting to their immediate circumstances. Tactics involving potential physical confrontation, in which emotions may run hot, seem to be no more likely to have breakdowns in nonviolent discipline than those which involve less potential for physical confrontation. This is not to deny the possibility that under certain circumstances an emotional response may drive a breakdown in nonviolent discipline. However, these kinds of gut responses do not appear to be the primary avenue through which breakdowns occur.

In terms of the theoretical framework presented in the previous section, the statistical analysis strongly supports the importance of the personal preferences for violent action and nonviolent action (the b_v and b_{nv} factors), and the influence of repression (the r_v and r_{nv} factors) on increasing or decreasing nonviolent discipline. From the statistical modeling it is less clear that the fear of campaign punishment plays a major role in inducing nonviolent discipline. The measures of campaign ability to punish and to communicate about punishment (hierarchy and internal unity) did not encourage nonviolent discipline but were actually associated with significantly more breakdowns in nonviolent discipline. While this testing is somewhat indirect, and thus does not rule out the possibility of campaign punishment or reward playing a role in encouraging nonviolent discipline, it does put it into doubt.

The major findings of the statistical research are summarized in Table 3 on the next page.

Table 3. Results of Statistical Analysis

History of Violent and Nonviolent Action?	Had an unclear effect on the whole group of campaigns, but may affect nonviolent discipline in large, revolutionary campaigns.
Wide Range of Previous Civil Resistance Tactics?	Had no measurable effect.
External Political Environment/ Concessions?	Had the opposite of the expected effect. Concessions to civil resistance campaigns were followed by breakdowns in nonviolent discipline.
Strong, Unified Campaign Leadership?	Had the opposite of the expected effect. Hierarchical, unified campaigns had lower nonviolent discipline.
Moderate Goals?	Had the expected effect. Campaigns with moderate goals had higher nonviolent discipline.
Tactical Choices to Avoid Confrontation?	Some weak indications that tactics with physical confrontation had lower NVD, but the results were unclear.
Diversity?	Had no measurable effect.
Repression?	Had the expected effect. Higher levels of repression of nonviolent actions led to declines in nonviolent discipline.
Membership Criteria?	Some weak indications of actions by youth having lower NVD, but the results were unclear.
Duration of Campaign?	Actions later in campaign had lower NVD, but the relationship was somewhat inconsistent.

Chapter 3
Comparing the Color Revolutions

This section builds on the findings in the statistical analysis and tests some of the expected influences on nonviolent discipline not amenable to statistical testing, with a structured, focused comparison of three influential cases of civil resistance:
- Serbia's "Bulldozer Revolution" in 2000,
- Georgia's "Rose Revolution" in 2003, and
- Kyrgyzstan's "Tulip Revolution" in 2005.

These three cases are examples of the wave of civil resistance movements in post-Communist countries in the early 2000s, popularly referred to as the "Color Revolutions." The fourth campaign typically included in this wave, Ukraine's "Orange Revolution," was not included because data from Ukraine were part of the statistical testing in the previous section.

These three cases were selected using a logic of "most similar systems," also known as Mill's "method of difference" (Mill 1856). This approach to case-study selection seeks to reproduce the conditions of a controlled experiment by choosing cases which are similar along many dimensions but vary along the dimension of particular interest, in this case levels of nonviolent discipline.

Cases from the Color Revolutions as opposed to three similar cases from other "waves" of civil resistance were chosen for several reasons. First, and most importantly, the cases showed a clear spectrum of variation in nonviolent discipline, as shown in Table 4. Second, the cases are from countries whose events are not included in the monograph's statistical testing. Third, recent cases were chosen rather than cases from older "waves" of civil resistance such as the anti-Communist movements of the late 1980s, with the goal of presenting analysis that is more directly relevant to practitioners of civil resistance today. Fourth, the cases in the Color Revolutions all followed similar strategic scripts, since activists from the earlier movements in the "wave" of revolutions, particularly the youth movement Otpor in Serbia, intentionally sought to share knowledge about civil resistance with activists in neighboring states. This pattern of diffusion and imitation, facilitated by the geographical and cultural proximity of the three cases, makes variation in nonviolent discipline all the more puzzling.

Table 4. *Color Revolution Comparison Snapshot*

Country, date	Campaign	Level of NVD
Serbia, 2000	Otpor/Bulldozer Revolution	Mostly Nonviolent
Georgia, 2003	Rose Revolution	Nearly Completely Nonviolent
Kyrgyzstan, 2005	Tulip Revolution	Barely Nonviolent

The examination of these cases uses George and Bennett's (2005) methods of process-tracing and structured, focused comparison. That is, the case studies focus on the particular configurations of the expected influences on nonviolent discipline in each campaign, looking for what degree each influence was present or absent, and carefully tracing the process from that influence to the outcome of stronger or weaker nonviolent discipline to determine its specific impacts.

The section presents a brief overview of the major events of each case, highlighting evidence on relative levels of nonviolent discipline and campaign and country attributes which relate to the expected influences on nonviolent discipline. After the brief narratives, the section discusses the similarities and differences across cases and presents evidence.[30]

Serbia: Bulldozers Not Bullets[31]

Popular opposition to Yugoslav President Slobodan Milosevic was relatively constant throughout the 1990s, beginning with student demonstrations in 1991 and

---

[30] Because many of the events related in the case summaries below are either common knowledge or were related by multiple sources, the section does not systematically provide in-text citations. Instead, the list of references at the conclusion of the monograph has a special section listing the major sources consulted to inform the case studies.

[31] The movement against Serbian President Milosevic was popularly referred to as the "Bulldozer Revolution" because in some of the final protests of the movement some activists used bulldozers to break down police barricades.

Chapter 3: Comparing the Color Revolutions

continuing as Yugoslavia gradually broke up from a six-republic federation to an ever-smaller rump state.

Local elections in 1996 provided a major locus for popular opposition. While the opposition swept many of the elections, Milosevic's ruling party refused to recognize the results, sparking nearly three months of popular protests. After severe violent repression and bloodshed, both sides achieved some victories and defeats. Milosevic recognized the opposition victories in many local elections but remained in power.

The civil resistance campaign that finally succeeded in ousting Milosevic from power can be traced to 1998, when a group of students, many of whom had been involved in the 1996 protests, came together to form Otpor ("Resistance") as a student organization with the explicit revolutionary goal of ousting Milosevic through an election and a planned campaign of civil resistance to ensure that the true results of the election were honored. Otpor's initial actions were small but savvy, drawing on street theater and humor to undermine the authority of the Milosevic regime and draw in popular interest.

Otpor and other Serbian civil society organizations benefited from extensive international financial and practical support, with leading Otpor activists receiving extensive training in the theory and practice of civil resistance. In addition, Otpor and other opposition activists received training and assistance from opposition activists who had been involved in nonviolent electoral defeats of semi-authoritarian leaders in Slovakia and Croatia that preceded the Serbian Bulldozer revolution.

Regime repression was consistent throughout Otpor's campaign. Police regularly

An Otpor sign near the University of Novi Sad, Serbia, in 2001.
Photo source: Wikimedia Commons, Joulupukki

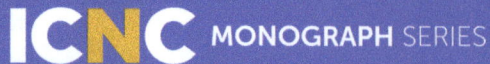

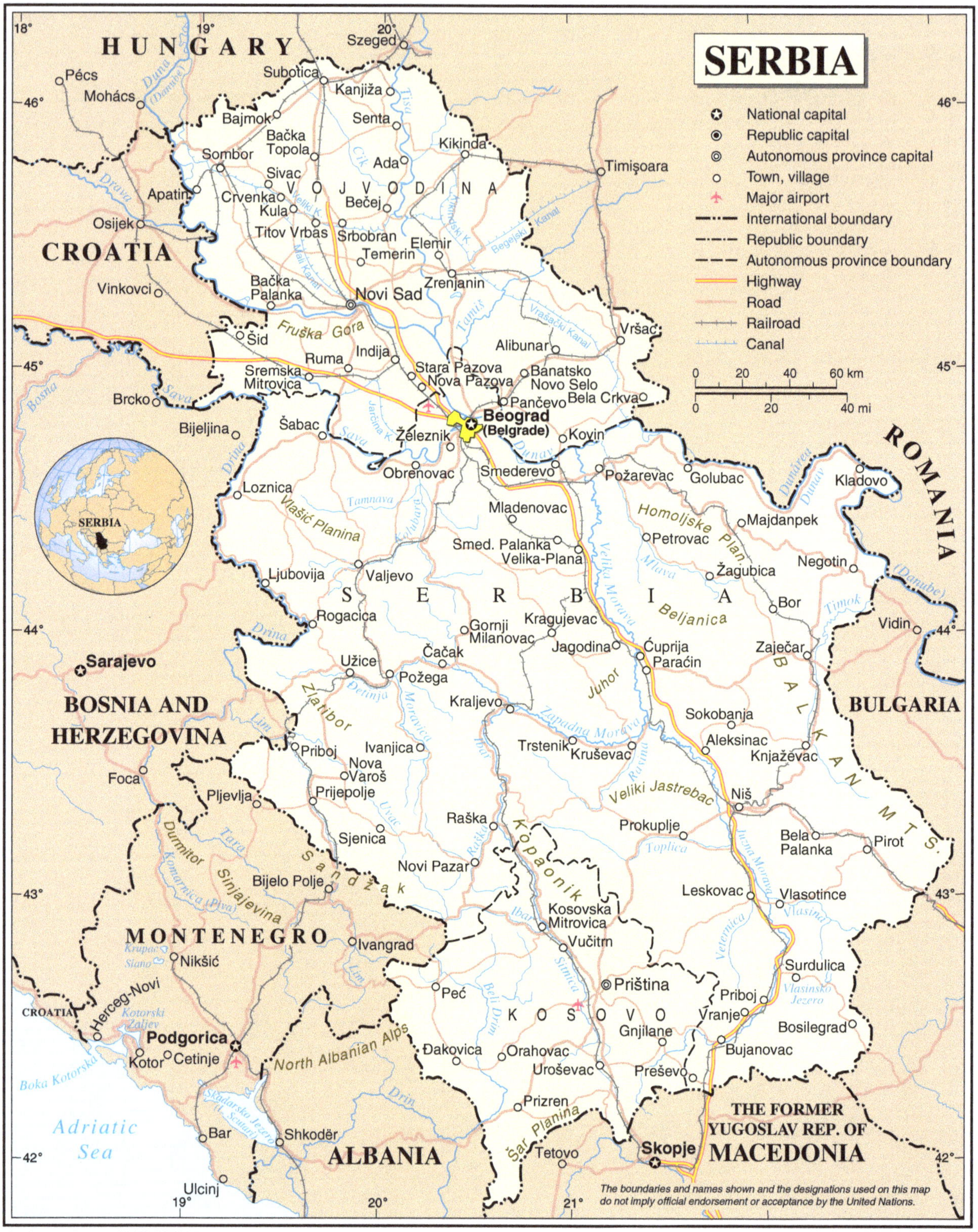

Map No. 4268 Rev.1 UNITED NATIONS
April 2007

Department of Peacekeeping Operation
Cartographic Section

Chapter 3: Comparing the Color Revolutions

arrested, intimidated or beat Otpor activists, and Milosevic's regime made repeated efforts to paint the organization as a subversive terrorist group. Throughout this early time Otpor's activists largely maintained nonviolent discipline, with few incidents of violence reported. This nonviolent discipline was widely reported to have been successful in turning Serbian public opinion against Milosevic, with the violent repression of students seen as a sign of regime weakness and thuggishness. Backlash against the regime violence and creative tactics helped Otpor grow rapidly, eventually reaching several thousand members in local branches throughout the country. Thus, in terms of diversity of participants, by the peak of its campaign activity, Otpor was extremely diverse along many different dimensions.

In 2000, President Milosevic announced that Serbia would hold early presidential elections in September of that year. Otpor activists, together with the formal political opposition, brought together in the alliance front "Democratic Opposition of Serbia" (DOS), began planning to use the election to orchestrate Milosevic's ouster. They expected that Milosevic would attempt to steal the election through rigging, but planned to expose the fraud through nationwide election monitoring, and to enforce the result through calling on people to protest until Milosevic stepped down.

In the first round of voting, while Milosevic admitted to not winning, he claimed that the opposition's candidate, Vosislav Kostunica, had also failed to gain a majority of votes, requiring a run-off election. However, the opposition's independent estimates showed that Kostunica had clearly won an absolute majority in the election.

In the days immediately following the first round of voting, DOS mapped out their strategy to bring down Milosevic. They called for a general strike and planned to have rural supporters from across Serbia converge on Belgrade on October 5th to paralyze the government. At these planning meetings the DOS leadership "unanimously decided to respond with whatever level of force was used against them by the police" (Bujosevic and Radovanovic 2003). Thus, while much of their public discourse emphasized civil disobedience they also stockpiled weapons and prepared special armed "task forces" led by former military or police members, to provide security and if necessary respond to police or military violence with force. Their guns, however, were never used due to the success of the nonviolent protests.

In the days leading up to October 5th, the most important group to join the general strike was coal miners at the Kolubara coal mine outside of Belgrade. Since the mine provided a large proportion of Serbia's electricity, the strike led to massive blackouts. The strike was meticulously organized, with workers occupying the mine and removing key pieces of machinery to prevent re-opening the mine using strikebreakers.

The night of October 4th, DOS leaders met with prominent security force leaders. Many in the security forces were unwilling or reluctant to defend the Milosevic regime but were concerned about violence from the opposition. DOS came to several informal agreements with security forces, promising to restrain protesters in exchange for security force restraint.

On October 5th across Serbia, supporters of DOS and Otpor began to march on Belgrade. In a critical blunder, the Serbian police were dispersed into a wide circle around the city, with only small detachments at roadblocks. These detachments were met by massive numbers of opposition supporters who demanded that police step aside. Nonviolent discipline was mixed, with some protesters passing through peacefully but others forcing police aside through physical violence or threats.

In Belgrade itself there were several violent clashes, some with improvised weapons, between police and protesters. However, while the government had ordered the police to prevent protesters from reaching Belgrade using rocket launchers and automatic weapons, police were unwilling to engage in high levels of violence. Thus, while elements of both sides were armed, opposition supporters largely followed the DOS decision to only respond to police violence with similar levels of force. While police attacked protesters with batons and tear gas, and protesters responded with stones, bottles and fists, there were few firefights. Overall violence on both sides was limited in scope and nature, particularly when considered in light of the overall scale and level of nonviolent discipline among hundreds of thousands that descended on the capital.

DOS and Otpor leaders also made a concerted effort to prevent violence, with several leaders making appeals to protesters to refrain from attacking police, and even physically intervening on occasion to prevent attacks on police from going too far.

By the end of the day the protesters were in control of the Serbian Parliament, state television and police stations. Many of the police and the state security special forces had joined (or defected to) the opposition, and armed DOS militia groups were guarding important points in Belgrade. The army, unwilling to fire on the Serbian people, largely stayed out of the fight. On October 6th Kostunica met with Milosevic, and Milosevic conceded the election.

The Bulldozer Revolution thus can be most accurately categorized as "mostly nonviolent" (refer to Table 4). Years of activism by Otpor were characterized by near-total nonviolent discipline. While breakdowns did occur in the final push to oust Milosevic, these were limited in scope and intensity. They were also fairly marginal relative to the massive numbers of protesters who converged on Belgrade. Thus it is accurate to describe this as a primarily nonviolent campaign, and as one displaying a high, yet imperfect degree of nonviolent discipline.

Georgia: Roses in Parliament

In 2003 the Georgian government prepared to hold parliamentary elections. Georgian President Eduard Shevardnadze had gradually grown unpopular due to widespread corruption and economic hardship. The Georgian opposition, previously fragmented into several disparate parties, saw an opportunity to shift control away from Shevardnadze and rallied to win a majority in Parliament.

Popular opposition in Georgia was not new. In the late 1980s and early 1990s Georgians had engaged in mass peaceful protests for independence from the Soviet Union. While the movement had been brutally repressed, they eventually succeeded in gaining Georgia's first multiparty elections in 1990 and independence from the Soviet Union in 1991.

> *When the threat of confrontation escalated during a march... opposition leaders called off the sit-in and instead urged their supporters to engage in a tax strike.*

In contrast to its largely peaceful move to independence, Georgia's brief post-Soviet history was deeply scarred by internal conflict. The region of South Ossetia waged a bloody struggle for autonomy from Georgia concurrently with the move towards Georgian independence, followed by another struggle for independence in the region of Abkhazia. Even more importantly, in late 1991 the violent dispersal of anti-government demonstrations led to a division in Georgian security forces, with armed government and opposition forces fighting in the street of Tbilisi. Independent Georgia's first president, Zviad Gamsakhurdia, was ousted shortly thereafter in a coup. Following his ouster, Gamsakhurdia waged a bloody civil war against the government until his defeat in 1993.

Almost a decade later, an attempt by President Shevardnadze to shut down an independent television station in 2001 had led to widespread peaceful protests which forced Shevardnadze to back down. Around the same time, former high-level regime

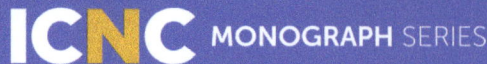

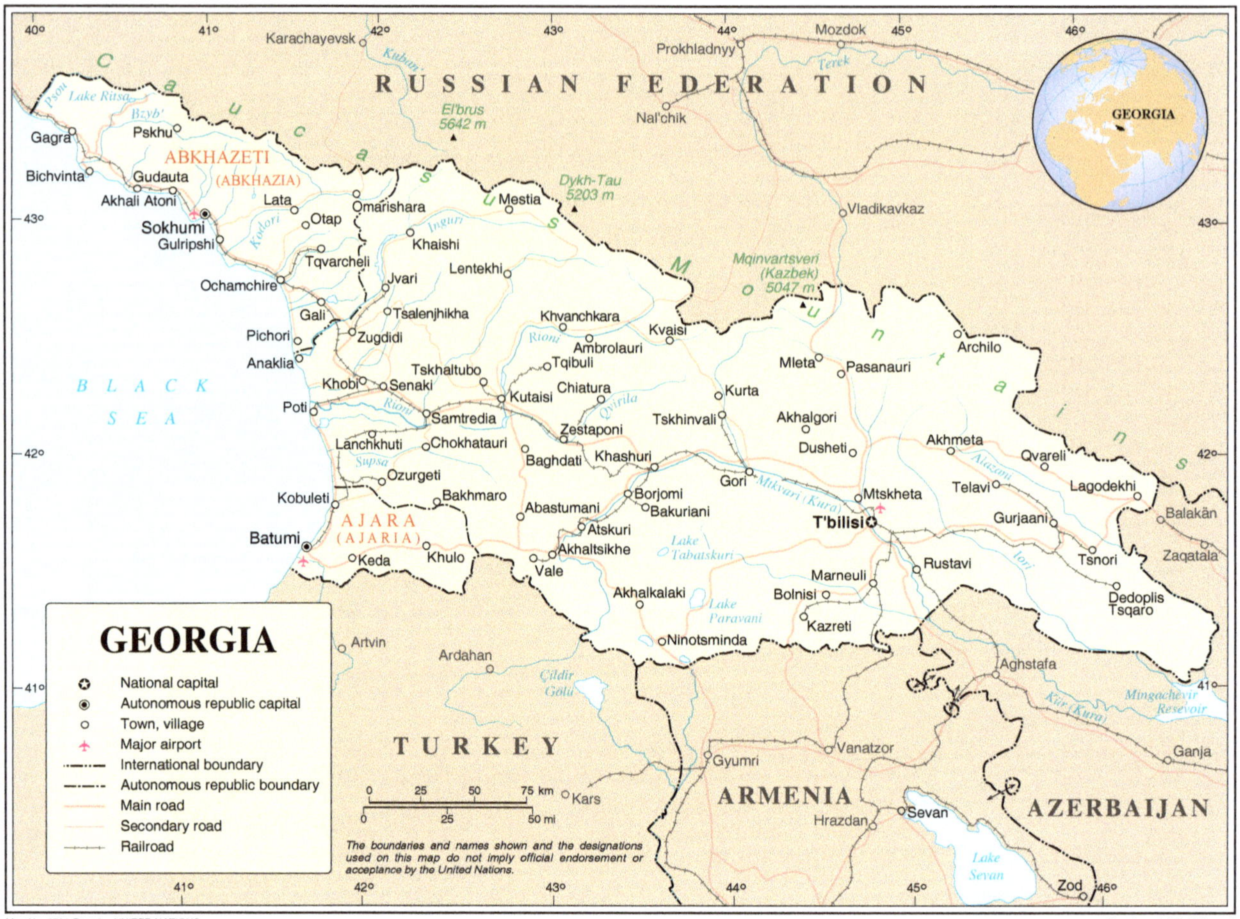

Map No. 3780 Rev. 6 UNITED NATIONS
September 2015

Department of Field Support
Geospatial Information Section (formerly Cartographic Section)

figure Michael Saakashvili had defected from the government and formed the opposition United National Movement (UNM). Saakashvili was a charismatic, youthful figure who promised major economic reforms.

Saakashvili and the other leaders of UNM, along with the reform-minded youth organization Kmara had been deeply inspired by the events of Serbia's 2000 Bulldozer Revolution. Saakashvili traveled to Serbia multiple times and received extensive training from Serbian opposition figures. Students in Kmara also attended "civil resistance summer camp" (Bunce and Wolchik 2011, 161) with leaders from Otpor, and very explicitly modeled their organization after Otpor.

In the lead-up to the elections, Saakashvili and the other opposition leaders faced violent harassment from security forces, and warned that there was a strong likelihood that the government would try to fake the election results. When the results seemed to show that Shevardnadze's party, along with a government-allied party led by a local

People organize in front of the Parliament building in Tbilisi, Georgia, in 2003.
Photo source: Wikimedia Commons, Zaraza

strongman, would dominate the Parliament, Saakashvili and the opposition immediately condemned the results as fraudulent and called on the Georgian people to peacefully protest to oust the government.

The campaign's goals were thus more reformist prior to the emergence of election fraud, focused on gaining a greater position in the Georgian Parliament. However, once the government's election fraud became apparent, they quickly shifted to the more revolutionary goal of fully ousting the Shevardnadze government.

The opposition and the regime both warned of the dangers of violence, issuing statements that invoked the memory of the civil war in the early 1990s. Shevardnadze attempted to deploy this discourse to dampen participation in the demonstrations, warning that the opposition was inevitably sending Georgia towards civil war. The opposition, on the other hand, constantly emphasized the fully peaceful nature of their struggle. Saakashvili in particular repeatedly called on his supporters to remain nonviolent, arguing that even a minor breach in nonviolent discipline would give the government "grounds for a provocation" (Mydans 2003). Kmara activists also attempted to encourage nonviolent discipline by fraternizing with soldiers, reducing the likelihood of repression and a violent escalation.

The campaign showed a great degree of tactical flexibility and willingness to adapt to changing circumstances. While the initial nonviolent action was a long-term sit-in outside of parliament, when the threat of confrontation escalated during a march towards the Presidential Palace, opposition leaders called off the sit-in and instead urged their supporters to engage in a tax strike and various other forms of noncooperation.

In late November 2003, when the final results of the parliamentary elections had been announced, definitively giving the victory to Shevardnadze, protests resumed and rapidly escalated throughout the country. As security forces refused to repress the demonstrations and many of Shevardnadze's top aides began to resign, Saakashvili led a group of protesters into the parliament building, disrupting a speech Shevardnadze was making to the opening session. The protesters carried roses in their hands to demonstrate their nonviolent intentions, a powerful symbol which gave the campaign the name Rose Revolution.

Shevardnadze fled and declared a state of emergency, but his security forces refused to comply with his orders. Both the United States and Russia, his two former major backers, called for a peaceful resolution to the conflict. Following Russian mediation, Shevardnadze announced his resignation. Presidential and parliamentary elections were held shortly thereafter, giving the opposition control of Parliament and propelling Saakashvili to the presidency.

Throughout the entire period of the Rose Revolution, very few if any breakdowns in nonviolent discipline were observed. Thus, as described in Table 4, this campaign is most accurately described as possessing near-perfect nonviolent discipline. While some minor infractions cannot be ruled out, in general, participants remained nonviolent for the duration of the campaign.

Kyrgyzstan: The Bloody Tulip

Protests in Kyrgyzstan began in early 2005 in the run-up to parliamentary elections. The recent uprisings in Georgia in 2003 and Ukraine in 2004 had rattled the regime of long-time president Askar Akayev. Akayev repeatedly warned the opposition that any attempt to oppose the government on the streets had the potential to quickly lead to civil and ethnic war. In the 1990s, political instability during the breakup of the Soviet Union had led to massive violence in the south of the country between the Kyrgyz majority and minority Uzbeks.

Since then the Akayev regime had been largely unopposed. Economic liberalization had created a class of economic elites independent of the regime, many of whom maintained political access through presence in Parliament. The opposition had only gone to the streets one time in 2002, when the arrest of opposition figure

Chapter 3: Comparing the Color Revolutions

Azimbek Beknazarov led his supporters in the region of Aksy to begin a campaign of demonstrations, strikes and road blockades to demand his release.

The Aksy campaign was violently repressed by state security forces. The government claimed they had only intervened when the demonstrations turned violent, while the opposition claimed that the government had repressed peaceful unarmed protesters. Yet while the campaign ended in repression it also gained concessions, as Beknazarov was released immediately afterwards.

Parliamentary elections in March 2005 were widely viewed as a lead-up to presidential elections later in the year. Akayev was required to step down following the elections due to term limits, but the opposition claimed he was attempting to hold onto power through fraudulently getting supporters into Parliament and appointing his children to high positions.

Former leaders of the Georgian Rose Revolution helped train the Kyrgyz opposition. Kyrgyz students also formed an anti-Akayev organization called Kelkel, modeled after Otpor, Kmara, and Pora (the youth organizations in Serbia, Georgia and Ukraine respectively). Yet the extent of this training appears to be somewhat limited, as opposed to the in-depth training given to Otpor and the leaders of the Rose Revolution.

Demonstrations were initiated prior to the actual elections, as local opposition elites in various districts, primarily in the south, mobilized their supporters to go to the streets to demand an end to alleged voter suppression and other forms of electoral manipulation by the regime. These initial protests started disparately, and focused on extremely localized grievances rather than revolutionary goals of ousting the Akayev regime. They were largely peaceful and did not face significant repression from the government.

A significant shift occurred when demonstrators in Jalalabad and Osh (see map above) moved from marches in the streets to occupying the regional government buildings in their cities. These dramatic seizures were at least partially forceful, though police largely did not resist. As these high profile actions began to draw greater attention to the movement, opposition elites throughout the country began quickly meeting to coordinate their efforts and articulate national-level goals.

Throughout the campaign, the opposition showed a high level of organization. Even in the first demonstrations, elites mobilized and organized their supporters, carefully planned actions, and policed them with self-defense groups intended to keep "order." As the initial protests began to network into a single unified campaign, the opposition also drew on local structures of traditional authority to create cells of support throughout the country with clear chains of command and accountability.

Nonviolent actions throughout also showed significant levels of diversity. While President Akayev had denounced the campaign early on by raising the specter of ethnic conflict, the opposition moved quickly to incorporate leaders from the country's large Uzbek minority. Demonstrations were also characterized by diverse participation in terms of gender, age, party and various other dimensions. Overall, the historical evidence suggests that the Tulip Revolution represented almost all major constituencies in Kyrgyzstan.

The opposition leadership did make some appeals for protesters to refrain from violence, and some protesters did replicate the tactic of carrying flowers to show their peaceful intentions, first tulips and later daffodils (Walsh 2005). However, several opposition leaders articulated a "tit for tat" logic to their peaceful behavior, urging followers to remain peaceful but threatening reprisals if police or the military cracked down on them.

Incidents of violence started small, with various scuffles occurring at demonstrations around the country, often attributed to protesters who were drunk. A major escalation occurred when the government dispatched police to remove the opposition supporters occupying the government buildings in Jalalabad and Osh. The occupiers fought back, resulting in some deaths on both sides. The following day the opposition engaged in a brutal push to oust the police from the buildings, resulting in some deaths, many injuries, and the destruction of the police station in Jalalabad.

As the opposition began to assume control over much of the country's periphery, leaders articulated demands for Akayev to step down. Several began organizing demonstrations outside the "White House" building, Kyrgyzstan's seat of government in Bishkek.

On March 24th, two columns of opposition supporters converged on the White House. Some reports describe a "vanguard" group of young protesters armed with batons and wooden shields who engaged in pitched battles with police, as well as hundreds of non-uniformed Akayev supporters, in an attempt to storm the building. After a battle of several hours between the two sides, the opposition supporters, who vastly outnumbered the police deployed outside the White House, broke through their lines and occupied the building, looting government property and smashing windows. Having lost much of the country, and with the seat of government in opposition's hands, Akayev fled the country and resigned 10 days later.

The evidence does indicate that the majority of demonstrators in Kyrgyzstan remained nonviolent, and thus it is accurate to describe the Tulip Revolution as a campaign of civil resistance. However, violent unarmed clashes were endemic to nearly the entire period of the campaign, and thus the level of nonviolent discipline can be best considered as extremely low, or "barely nonviolent."

Table 5. Main Findings from Case Comparison

Influences	Georgia Relevant	Georgia Effects	Serbia Relevant	Serbia Effects	Kyrgyzstan Relevant	Kyrgyzstan Effects
Historical Conflict	Yes	Past civil war invoked to maintain NVD	Yes	Past conflicts prevented repression	Yes	Helped prevent ethnic violence, did not help NVD
Information/ Training	Yes	Training kept group nonviolent	Yes	Effective in core, not larger population	Yes	No apparent effects
Wide Range of Past Civil Resistance Tactics	No	No major past civil resistance campaigns	Yes	Wide range of past tactics, but no full NVD	No	No major past civil resistance campaigns
Favorable External Environment	Yes	Prior protests led to some concessions	No	Prior protests were repressed	Mixed	Prior protests led to repression
Appeals for Nonviolent Discipline?	Yes	Consistent appeals helped	Mixed	Unclear standards led to clashes	No	Leaders encouraged some violence
Centralized Leadership	Yes	Encouraged NVD	Yes	Called for only responsive violence	Yes	Encouraged violence
Moderate Goals	No	Extreme goals didn't lead to violence	No	Extreme goals led to some violence	Yes	Violence increased with extreme goals
Tactics to Avoid Confrontation	Yes	Avoided clashes	Mixed	Violence during physical confrontations	No	"Holding territory" led to violent clashes
Membership Criteria	Unclear	No evidence of membership criteria	Mixed	NVD broke down after becoming mass movement	No	Youth committed to violence were recruited
Diversity	Yes	No observed effect	Yes	No observed effect	Yes	No observed effect
Campaign Punishment	No	No major violations of NVD	Yes	Leaders broke up scuffles and condemned	No	Leaders encouraged violence
Repression	Minor	No major repression of protesters	Mixed	Violence followed police repression	Yes	Police attacks sparked major clashes
Duration	No	No major violence	Yes	Violence occurred late in campaign	Yes	Violence occurred in mid to late campaign

Chapter 4
Case Study Discussion

How does the evidence from these cases support or undermine the various expected influences on nonviolent discipline? The findings of the case studies are summarized in Table 5 in the previous chapter, while the following section briefly considers what cross-case comparison, as well as in-case process-tracing, can tell us about the various influences argued to support or undermine nonviolent discipline.

Historical Experience

In all three cases, historical experience of violent conflict played a key role. In Serbia, the shadow of the recent Balkan wars loomed large in the minds of DOS and Otpor. Perhaps even more critically, this historical experience was fresh in the minds of security forces, who feared a popular rebellion would spark NATO intervention (Bujosevic and Radovanovic 2003, 11). In Georgia, the civil war between supporters of President Gamsakhurdia and Shevardnadze in the early 1990s, as well as the separatist conflicts in Abkhazia and South Ossetia encouraged significant restraint on both sides. Early demonstrations that had successfully led to Georgian independence were also cited as demonstrating the power of nonviolent action to achieve change. And in Kyrgyzstan, the memory of ethnic conflict in the 1990s motivated the opposition to quickly incorporate Uzbeks into their anti-Akayev alliance.

The levels of nonviolent discipline in the three cases link quite closely to how "central" the previous violent conflicts had been. In Kyrgyzstan, the ethnic conflict of the 1990s had been peripheral, with control of the state never in question. In Serbia, while the array of Balkan conflicts in the 1990s had no doubt been an existential threat to the previous Yugoslavia, intra-Serb conflict had been minimal and Serbian opposition forces had not taken up arms against the government. Finally, in Georgia, the civil war had been a core, existential threat to the country, with tanks and armed struggle in the

streets of Tbilisi. The "centrality" of armed conflict thus appears to be a factor mediating the direct impact of a history of violent conflict in strengthening nonviolent discipline.

Training and Information on Past Civil Resistance Campaigns

Experience of and information on previous nonviolent struggles also appeared to have important impacts, though they were inconsistent in producing nonviolent discipline. In all three cases campaign leaders were exposed to significant amounts of information on past civil resistance campaigns and received training in civil resistance. In Kyrgyzstan in particular, recent successful campaigns in Georgia and Ukraine were powerful frames which the opposition drew on. Yet their training and the recent powerful examples of successful nonviolent resistance did not motivate the Kyrgyz opposition to enforce higher levels of nonviolent discipline.

Why is this the case? One potential explanation has to do with the quality of training, and the particular lessons that campaign leaders take from recent experiences. While Kyrgyz leaders did receive some training in civil resistance, the evidence indicates that this training was fairly limited. This contrasts with both the Serbian and the Georgian cases, in which training in civil resistance was extensive and detailed. With such limited training, it is questionable whether leaders in the Tulip Revolution had a very sophisticated understanding of the dynamics of nonviolent action. Instead, their tactical choices appear to have been driven by a vaguer feeling, based on the experience of the previous Color Revolutions, that ousting a dictator was a simple matter of bringing large numbers of protesters onto the streets. Dynamics of civil resistance such as the importance of nonviolent discipline were poorly understood and thus poorly implemented. Thus, the impact of training and exposure to information on past nonviolent struggles in these cases, while real, appears to be mediated by the quality of the training and information to which campaign leaders and participants are exposed.

Wide Range of Past Civil Resistance Tactics

The existence of a wide range of past civil resistance tactics appears to have had an inconsistent impact in these three cases. The case with the widest range of previously used tactics was likely Serbia, where past opposition activity and Otpor's years of innovation had developed a complex, detailed set of different civil resistance tactics. Yet this high degree of tactical diversity did not translate to higher nonviolent discipline than, say, in Georgia, where near-perfect nonviolent discipline was maintained despite a much less complex and robust set of civil resistance tactics available from their country's historical experience.

Previous Political Concessions

While evidence on the more immediate impact of concessions is unclear, in the longer term it seems that concessions were related to higher levels of nonviolent discipline. In both Georgia and Serbia nonviolent movements in the recent past had led to some concessions, with Milosevic allowing opposition figures to assume some rural positions following demonstrations in 1996; and Shevardnadze had re-opened an independent TV station in 2001 following protests. In contrast, in Kyrgyzstan the Aksy campaign, while successful in gaining the freedom of Beknazarov, had also led to significant repression.

This relationship contrasts with the finding from the statistical analysis that concessions are associated with higher levels of breakdown in nonviolent discipline. However, the time frames for these concessions (several years before the campaign) are different from the time frames examined in the quantitative data, which focused more on concessions in response to more recent nonviolent actions. Thus, concessions in the longer term may be associated with higher levels of nonviolent discipline because of the increased general feeling that civil resistance succeeds, while concessions in the short term decrease nonviolent discipline because of campaign overconfidence, as discussed in the statistical analysis.

Appeals from Movement Leaders for Nonviolent Discipline

The three cases closely follow the expected influence of appeals from movement leaders for nonviolent discipline, with stronger and more consistent appeals leading to greater nonviolent discipline. In Georgia, campaign leadership consistently presented a message of purely nonviolent resistance. In Serbia, the messaging was mixed. Portions of the campaign, such as Otpor, were committed to a civil resistance strategy. When

they dominated the campaign, nonviolent discipline was extremely high. Yet the DOS leadership was prepared to make "proportional responses" to security force violence. Finally, in Kyrgyzstan, the primary locus of opposition was generally united around a strategy of using peaceful tactics until the regime responded with violence, and then shifting to violent tactics.

Strong, Cohesive Campaign Leadership

All three campaigns quickly developed a strong cohesive leadership. Indeed, the Kyrgyz case may have been the "strongest" of the three, as traditional forms of governance and organization were rapidly appropriated by the opposition. The fact that this high level of hierarchy and structure were accompanied with violence supports the statistical finding that non-hierarchical campaigns tend to have greater nonviolent discipline. However, because hierarchy was to some extent present in all three campaigns, it is difficult to judge its impact.

Moderate Strategic Goals

The expected influence of moderate goals in support of nonviolent discipline also receives some limited support. In all three cases the campaigns quickly articulated revolutionary goals. However, in Kyrgyzstan early on in the campaign, when goals were limited to demands for localized election recounts, campaign actions remained more peaceful. Levels of violence increased as the campaign shifted focus to ousting Akayev. However, sources are unclear as to whether the increase in violence was directly connected to the escalating demands (goals) of the campaign.

Tactical Choices to Avoid Confrontation

Tactical choices to avoid or encourage confrontation are also a key point of differentiation. In particular, breakdowns in nonviolent discipline closely correlated with strategies which relied on "holding territory."

These tactics of intervention were prominent early on in Kyrgyzstan, when opposition protesters in Osh and Jalalabad violently occupied regional government buildings. Holding these physical sites became a core aspect of the campaign's strategy, sparking a violent repressive response and then responsive violence by the opposition bound to "retake" lost ground. Similarly, in Serbia, the primary locus of violence occurred when protesters attempted to occupy the parliament, state TV stations, and other physical spaces.

Breakdowns in nonviolent discipline closely correlated with strategies that relied on "holding territory."

In Georgia, in contrast, maintaining occupation of physical space was never central to the movement's strategy. Instead they tended to withdraw from particular spaces when threatened with confrontation. The one highly visible and symbolic confrontational occupation of physical space—Saakashvili's entrance into the parliament—was brief and only undertaken when regime support was already breaking down.

Membership Criteria Excluding Violent Actors

Variation within individual campaigns in response to repression points to the importance of campaign membership criteria. In Serbia, for example, while violent repression had been relatively consistent for years, these early instances of repression against a small, better-trained group of student activists did not lead to breakdowns in nonviolent discipline. The repression-violence dynamic only came into play when participation extended from the core group of activists to hundreds of thousands of protesters.

This suggests that exclusion and repression have an interactive relationship. Nonviolent discipline in the face of repression may be maintained with a smaller, more selective campaign base, but when the campaign reaches a larger size, repression more directly leads to breakdowns in nonviolent discipline.

A key challenge is thus how to spread nonviolent discipline from a committed core group to the larger population, and campaign leaders must weigh the potential for breakdowns in nonviolent discipline with a larger participant body against the strategic benefits to be gained from a campaign of larger size.

This question may relate to the particular phase of the civil resistance campaign. In the early phase, when the campaign is dominated by a small group of committed activists, maintaining nonviolent discipline may be less challenging. However, when the campaign reaches its peak and participation becomes much higher, discipline is a greater challenge. The key variation is thus which campaigns are able to keep nonviolent discipline even through the peak of their campaign. While the evidence from the cases is inconclusive on this point, intuitively one might speculate that timing and speed of campaign growth could play a role here. If a campaign moves rapidly from an early growth phase to a peak of activity, the transition from a committed core group to a large popular uprising may lead to breakdowns in nonviolent discipline. Further examination of this question will be a fruitful area for future research.

The role of "armed wings" is brought into question in an interesting way in comparing these three campaigns. Armed groups were connected to the civil resistance campaigns in both the Serbian case and the Kyrgyz case, even though they consisted primarily of unarmed participants. In Kyrgyzstan these groups were directly integrated with the unarmed protesters and clashed violently with security forces in several circumstances. In Serbia, on the other hand, armed guards from DOS were only deployed as a way to maintain stability and public security after the main confrontation had passed.

While it is difficult to say with certainty, these groups may have helped maintain nonviolent discipline in this final stage by preventing the emergence of a security vacuum. However, their existence also speaks to the willingness of DOS to use violence if violence was used against them, a factor which may have undermined nonviolent discipline during the peak phase of the movement.

High Levels of Diversity

Diversity did not appear to make a difference in any of these three cases. While the campaigns tended to start with a less diverse group, particularly in Serbia and Georgia, by their peak all three showed evidence of high degrees of diversity along any number of dimensions (age, gender, region, political party). While in Georgia this highly diverse group maintained very high nonviolent discipline, in Kyrgyzstan they engaged in significant levels of violence. While more fine-grained information might reveal some impacts of diversity, the case study research at this level was unable to determine any influence.

Campaign Punishment for Violent Actions

Campaign punishment did appear to have an effect on nonviolent discipline. For this expected influence, the comparison between Serbia and Kyrgyzstan is most relevant. In Serbia, while the opposition leadership was encouraging some degree of preparation for a violent response to the regime, opposition and Otpor leaders also intervened and condemned protesters who "went too far" during violent confrontations. While the level of punishment was fairly minimal, there was at least some sense of a possibility to be punished for behavior in case protesters' actions went beyond the campaign's acceptable level of violence. In Kyrgyzstan, in contrast, campaign leaders not only let violence go unpunished, but actively encouraged certain levels of violence.

Repression of Nonviolent Action

Repression had a clear impact, with a very close correlation between patterns of repression and breakdowns in nonviolent discipline. In Georgia, while violent repression did occur it was always very narrowly targeted at campaign leaders. In Serbia, security forces refrained from extreme violence towards protesters, but they did attack them with tear gas and batons, sparking violent clashes. Finally, in Kyrgyzstan, police and government supporters engaged in pitched battles with the opposition.

Finally, breakdowns in nonviolent discipline did become more prevalent in both campaigns that had significant incidents of violence. Nearly all of the breakdowns in nonviolent discipline in Serbia occurred on the very last day of the campaign, when hundreds of thousands of protesters descended on Belgrade. Violence in Kyrgyzstan was very minimal in early demonstrations, only became serious midway through the campaign, and peaked at the very end of the campaign with the major clashes outside of the White House in Bishkek.

The campaign with the highest level of nonviolent discipline, Georgia, was also the shortest of the three campaigns, with only roughly three weeks of major activity before Shevardnadze stepped down. In contrast, the campaign in Serbia had been ongoing for several years, and protests in Kyrgyzstan lasted several months.

The relationship between the length of the campaign and breakdowns in nonviolent discipline is not simple and direct. The Serbian campaign, for instance, was

much longer than the Kyrgyz campaign, yet had much higher levels of nonviolent discipline. However, the general pattern of the three campaigns does suggest that breakdowns in nonviolent discipline tend to occur more and more frequently as civil resistance campaigns progress.

Table 6 (on the following page) summarizes and simplifies the findings from the comparative case study and compares them with the findings from the statistical analysis. There are some points of divergence, for instance regarding the effects of concessions and a favorable external environment. Concessions generally correlated with higher nonviolent discipline in the case studies, but lower nonviolent discipline in the statistical testing. However, as discussed above, this seems to be a question of timing, with the statistical tests measuring more immediate concessions and the case studies looking at a longer time frame. The effect of revolutionary goals also diverged slightly in the case studies, with the revolutionary Rose Revolution nonetheless having very high nonviolent discipline. This illustrates that while revolutionary goals may make it harder to maintain nonviolent discipline, as shown in the statistical findings, this is still possible if other factors such as consistent campaign appeals for strict nonviolent discipline are present. Overall, the findings of the case-study comparison complement and deepen the findings of the statistical analysis and point to consistent patterns of influence in several of the ways predicted by the theory of nonviolent discipline described by the first section of the monograph.

Chapter 4: Case Study Discussion

Table 6. *Case Comparison and Statistics Findings*

Influences	Georgia	Serbia	Kyrgyzstan	Statistical Results
Historical Conflict	Increased NVD	Increased NVD	No apparent effect	Weak increase
Information/ Training	Increased NVD	Increased NVD	Did not increase NVD	N/A
Past Civil Resistance Tactics	N/A	Weak increase	N/A	No effect
Favorable External Environment	Increased NVD	Increased NVD	N/A	N/A
Appeals for NVD	Increased NVD	Weak increase	Not present	N/A
Centralized Leadership	Increased NVD	Mixed effects	Decreased NVD	Decreased NVD
Moderate Goals	Extreme goals yet high NVD	Unclear	Increased NVD	Increased NVD
Tactics to Avoid Confrontation	Increased NVD	Increased NVD	N/A	Weak increase
Membership Criteria	N/A	Increased NVD when present	Not present	N/A
Diversity	No observed effect	No observed effect	No observed effect	No effect
Campaign Punishment	N/A	Weak increase	No punishment	N/A
Repression	N/A	Decreased NVD	Decreased NVD	Decreased NVD
Duration	N/A	Decreased NVD	Decreased NVD	Weak decrease

Conclusion: Applied Learning on Nonviolent Discipline

This monograph has presented a unified theory of nonviolent discipline, relying on a simple mathematical model and insights from the selected literature on civil resistance to produce expected influences likely to create and sustain nonviolent discipline. The monograph has also tested the impact of these expected influences using data from the NAVCO 3.0 dataset and three comparative case studies. This final section summarizes the major findings from that testing and presents some "take-away" lessons for academics, activists and outside professionals in civil society and the policy-making world.

Scholar-Relevant Findings

For researchers and academics, it is hoped that this monograph will spark new studies on the dynamics of the various factors influencing nonviolent discipline in civil resistance movements. Both the statistical testing and case study analysis represent first cuts at this important question, leaving several open and interesting questions. For instance, the finding that campaign unity only appears to impact nonviolent discipline if there is consistent messaging and a clear commitment to nonviolent action on the part of campaign leaders could be a fruitful area for further examination.

Crucial questions remain to be answered in regard to how nonviolent discipline is initially created. The monograph's theory assumes a situation in which campaign leaders have called upon their followers to remain nonviolent. Yet this initial choice by campaign leaders is a major unresolved question. The growing research program seeking to address this question[32] could benefit from incorporating aspects of the findings from this monograph, such as the importance of differences in leadership's levels of commitment to nonviolent action. The focus on nonviolent discipline also suggests

---

[32] See for example Asal et al 2013, Bakke 2010, Cunningham 2013, Lawrence 2010, Pearlman 2011.

the value of examining this question in terms of an ongoing process of maintaining or degrading a campaign's strategy of contention.

The finding on the superior levels of nonviolent discipline in non-hierarchical campaigns also opens the door for significant additional research. Wendy Pearlman's (2011) argument that a unified, centralized campaign structure is necessary to remain nonviolent has been very influential in the field. How can her findings be reconciled with the data showing that non-hierarchical campaigns with some internal conflict have greater nonviolent discipline? While this monograph has offered some theoretically-informed speculation as to why this relationship occurs, more research is needed to tease out these causal mechanisms and understand under what conditions they will be influential.

> *The finding on the superior levels of nonviolent discipline in non-hierarchical campaigns opens the door for significant additional research.*

The surprising finding that concessions are associated with greater breakdowns in nonviolent discipline strongly calls for more research. While this monograph has offered some thoughts on why this relationship might so consistently occur, informed by the research of scholars such as Kathleen Cunningham (2013, 2014), these thoughts remain highly speculative. In-depth qualitative research of campaigns in the times immediately following concessions could help flesh out why this relationship occurs.

Past experiences of violent and nonviolent conflict do seem to be important, but their impact is not consistent, as shown in the statistics and in the case studies. While past experiences certainly inform the calculus of campaign and regime leaders, their effects are subtle. One particular aspect of history shown in the cases, and which merits further scholarly examination, is the centrality and brutality of past violent conflict in encouraging nonviolent discipline. Further research into how the particular characteristics of past violent and nonviolent campaigns influence future patterns of violent and nonviolent action would be beneficial.

The theory's strong individualistic basis also suggests that future research on nonviolent discipline that starts at the individual level could be fruitful. A first step here would be to generate individual values for the various factors included in the mathematical model such as individual preferences for nonviolent and violent action (the b_{nv} and b_v factors). Survey research, or in-depth individual interviews with participants in civil resistance campaigns would be good methods of generating this information.

Conclusion: Applied Learning on Nonviolent Discipline

Collecting this individual-level information could then provide an entry point for seeing how various influences directly impact these personal preferences for each individual participant in a campaign.

Direct studies on the impact of training in effective civil resistance would be beneficial for understanding how nonviolent discipline is both created and sustained. The evidence from the case studies suggested that the impact of training is likely mediated by its depth and quality. Yet the evidence presented here is only suggestive, leaving many additional questions open. What aspects of training in civil resistance are particularly crucial in encouraging nonviolent discipline? Is it more important, for example, to train campaign leaders in the general dynamics of civil resistance, or to give campaign participants hands-on experience in responding nonviolently to repression? Can a brief lecture-style training session impact the conduct of a civil resistance campaign? Or is a longer, more intensive training regimen necessary before impacts on campaign behavior can be observed? Several organizations, such as the Center for Applied Nonviolent Action and Strategies (CANVAS), the International Center for Nonviolent Conflict (ICNC), and Rhize engage in various forms of civil resistance training. Better understanding of how differing models of training impact nonviolent discipline could provide an important scholarly contribution to their efforts.

Finally, while the monograph has examined a large number of potential influences, this set is by no means complete. A number of additional factors not examined in this research may plausibly exert consistent and reliable impacts on nonviolent discipline.

One important avenue to explore would be the effects of gender on nonviolent discipline.[33] While women's contributions have too often gone unrecognized, their participation has been critical in the origins, development and success of many civil resistance campaigns (McAllister 1988). From inspirational leaders such as Corazon Aquino in the Philippines and Tawakkol Karman in Yemen to bold movement pioneers such as Rosa Parks in the United States or the Mothers of the Plaza de Mayo in Argentine, the story of civil resistance has often been the story of women. Furthermore, as Codur and King observe, in many movements "women are often the best keepers of nonviolent discipline" (Codur and King 2014, 433). While the complexities of gender norms will no doubt vary depending on the cultural context, women may in many situations

---

[33] Thanks to an anonymous reviewer for suggesting this.

be less prone to a male-based "warrior culture" that encourages violent responses to injustices (Bartkowski 2013). Thus they may be more resilient in maintaining nonviolent discipline. Exploring the specific effects of gender on nonviolent discipline, as well as the strategic advantages granted to civil resistance by facilitating gender diversity is a crucial question requiring further examination.

Another important potential influence not modeled in this research is the effect of other campaign participants' behavior.[34] While the monograph examines the effects of leaders' behavior, individual activists may also be powerfully affected by the choices of the other activists in the campaign.

> *Repression makes maintenance of nonviolent discipline while in the midst of a civil resistance mobilization an ongoing challenge, leading to breakdowns in the processes of civil resistance*

Maintaining nonviolent discipline will likely be much easier if everyone around you is doing the same. Thus each individual's choice to maintain nonviolent discipline may not be equally likely, but rather patterns of nonviolent discipline and its breakdowns may follow cascading patterns as individual campaign participants follow the lead of their peers. This could be particularly important in relation to the finding that non-hierarchical campaigns tend to have higher nonviolent discipline, as the lack of a hierarchical structure might allow for greater peer influence to come to the fore.

Activist-Relevant Findings

For organizers engaged in civil resistance, the most important and consistent finding from both the quantitative and qualitative testing is the challenge of repression. Nonviolent discipline tends to break down most commonly and most dramatically in civil resistance actions following violent repression. While this may be unsurprising to activists, it does suggest something of a twist on the traditional story told by critics of nonviolent action. It is not that civil resistance fails to achieve success, steering nonviolent dissidents to choose violent tactics. Rather, repression makes maintenance of nonviolent discipline while in the midst of a civil resistance mobilization an ongoing challenge, leading to breakdowns in the processes of civil resistance.

---

[34] Thanks to Brian Martin for suggesting this potential influence.

Conclusion: Applied Learning on Nonviolent Discipline

The statistical evidence did suggest another variation on a common story told about the relationship between repression and weakening of nonviolent discipline. Breakdowns in nonviolent discipline do not tend to happen immediately following repression, but instead become more likely when repression is sustained over many past nonviolent actions. This suggests that breakdowns in nonviolent discipline following repression, on average, are not simply *ad hoc*, spontaneous "lashing out" but rather represent more predictable long-term responses to the changing, more violent, political environment. This indirectly and somehow optimistically suggests that activists might have time—possibly counted in weeks and months—to readjust their strategies before the breakdown in nonviolent discipline as a result of repression becomes the reality.

The clear question then is what campaigns can do to avoid activating this repression-breakdown of nonviolent discipline/takeover-by-violence dynamic. In this regard, the quantitative evidence indicates that campaign characteristics such as hierarchy and visible unity may actually be counterproductive. Instead, non-hierarchical campaigns which allowed visible disagreements over matters of policy or ideology contributed to the maintenance of higher levels of nonviolent discipline. This suggests that campaigns where individual participants have greater ownership, rather than simply following orders, may incentivize activists to remain nonviolent. Organizers and practitioners who wish to motivate their followers to remain nonviolent would be wise to focus on building inclusive structures that generate a proprietary feeling and allow disagreements to be debated and threshed out, rather than suppressed.

The evidence from the case studies is helpful in further clarifying this picture. In all three cases, centralized, hierarchical leadership only helped produce nonviolent discipline when that leadership itself was clearly and consistently committed to maintaining a purely nonviolent strategy. A leadership may be highly centralized and have few internal conflicts, as in Kyrgyzstan, but this does not encourage nonviolent discipline if the leadership is not fully committed to nonviolent resistance.

The surprising finding that concessions are associated with more breakdowns in nonviolent discipline provides a caution to practitioners of nonviolent action. While the specific implications of the finding remain ambiguous, as mentioned above, and more research is needed, the strong statistical robustness of the finding indicates that this is a genuine, consistent pattern across many different campaigns, and thus something which activists should be generally aware of and take care to prepare for. Campaigns that achieve concessions should be careful not to "rest on their laurels," or be unnecessarily celebratory in ways that might cause them to lose focus. Instead they should continue to ensure they are doing all in their power to maintain momentum, unity and nonviolent discipline. They should also be careful that concessions do not lead to demobilizing moderates, or create divisions within the movement that may give more radical and violent groups a freer hand to pursue violent tactics (Cunningham 2014). Developing strategies to prepare for these potential negative effects of concessions is critical for movements seeking to maintain nonviolent discipline.

In regard to particular tactics, some minor statistical evidence does appear to show that strikes are less likely than protests or sit-ins to lead to breakdowns in nonviolent discipline, but this evidence is fairly weak. Tying this evidence with the case studies, however, a clearer picture emerges. Choosing tactics to avoid direct physical confrontation is not a simple matter of choosing between "strikes or sit-ins." There is no tactical "one-size-fits-all" solution to promoting nonviolent discipline. Rather, tactical choices will be deeply contextual. As in Georgia, physically confrontational tactics may be more appropriate when one is more confident that security forces will not use violent repression, while when repression is likely, it may be wise to pull back from confrontational interventions and rely on tactics of noncooperation and dispersion.

Findings for Civil Society and Policymakers

Finally, what do the findings of this monograph have to offer external civil society or policymaking professionals, in particular those who may be called upon to offer assistance to civil resistance campaigns?

First, the findings of the monograph suggest that training in civil resistance should be carefully planned and considered. Simply facilitating the spread of information may be insufficient to communicate crucial messages such as the importance of nonviolent discipline. Instead, external actors interested in spreading knowledge about civil resistance should be careful to encourage more detailed and comprehensive training.

Second, the findings on repression reiterate the importance of pressuring regimes that do not respect their people's rights of free association through methods such as shaming and the threat or use of sanctions, specifically when governments use violence against unarmed, peaceful protesters. Critically, even moderate decreases in the frequency and intensity of repression could have important positive impacts on movements. Thus, diplomats, international human rights activists and others should

Conclusion: Applied Learning on Nonviolent Discipline

not lose hope if they are unable to fully prevent repression of peaceful civil resistance. Even marginal gains can lead to significantly fewer breakdowns in nonviolent discipline among activists, and thus more peaceful and transformative domestic politics.

Third, if international actors are in a position to assist civil resistance campaigns, they should do it early. Or at least, they should not wait until the campaign has been ongoing for a long period of time. The longer campaigns continue, the more likely breakdowns in nonviolent discipline become.

> *If international actors are in a position to assist civil resistance campaigns, they should do it early.*

Fourth, the findings of the monograph would suggest that, when evaluating which movements to support, outside actors should not be too quick to dismiss those that may lack a hierarchical structure or that have significant internal disagreements. While it may be more difficult for external actors to interact with movements without a single leader and hierarchical structure, these campaigns may actually be more likely to remain nonviolent and thus effective in the long term.

The study of civil resistance remains in its early stages, and much remains unclear or ambiguous. Yet in a time of possibly resurgent authoritarianism (Burrows and Stephan 2015), understanding the challenges and potentials of civil resistance and the driving force of nonviolent discipline is more important than ever. It is the hope of the author that this monograph may contribute even in some small way to building complex knowledge that can be used to encourage freedom and justice.

Appendix A: Statistical Annex

This statistical annex provides details on the operationalization of variables used in the statistical testing section, details on the methods of statistical testing and their justification, as well as a more technical presentation of the various robustness checks run to ensure that the relationships identified in that section were not spurious. The annex will be of interest to quantitatively-minded academics interested in the details of the testing procedures, as well as anyone with questions or concerns about the structure of the statistical testing.

The data for the statistical tests are drawn from the Nonviolent and Violent Campaigns and Outcomes (NAVCO) 3.0 dataset, the latest iteration of the ongoing NAVCO data project.[35] NAVCO 3.0 collects information on political contention in several countries globally from 1991 to 2012. In contrast to previous iterations of the NAVCO data, NAVCO 3.0 is highly disaggregated, with individual events coded separately rather than aggregated into campaigns or campaign-years.

Statistical testing involved the individual event as the unit of analysis, with nonviolent discipline measured as whether a particular event, nested in a nonviolent campaign, involved violent action. While campaign attributes are included in the model as independent variables, the dependent variable is thus not, for instance, an average "nonviolent discipline" score for a campaign, but rather the likelihood that a particular event will be violent.

The basic coding structure of the data follows the CAMEO coding scheme of "Actors" performing "Verbs" against "Targets."[36] In NAVCO each of these three categories can have up to three levels of possible specificity. To illustrate, Table 1 below presents a typical line of NAVCO 3.0 core code. This particular line represents student protesters (ACT STU) engaging in a protest or demonstration for policy change (1412) against the ministry of education (GOV EDU).

---

[35] For more information on the project, see www.navcodata.org and also Erica Chenoweth and Orion Lewis "Unpacking Nonviolent Campaigns: Introducing the NAVCO 2.0 Data," *Journal of Peace Research* 50.3 (2013).

[36] Phillip A. Schrodt, "CAMEO: Conflict and Mediation Event Observations Event and Actor Codebook," *Computational Event Data Systems* (2012).

Statistical Annex

Table 1. *Case Comparison and Statistics Findings*

actor_3	actor_6	actor_9	verb_10	verb_100	verb_1000	target_3	target_6	target_9
ACT	STU		14	141	1412	GOV	EDU	

In addition to the core Actor-Verb-Target data, NAVCO 3.0 includes a wide number of additional variables coding elements such as the specific location, numbers of participants, and levels of government repression (see Table 1). For a full listing of auxiliary variables, see the NAVCO 3.0 codebook.

Events are disaggregated by actors, verbs and targets. For example, different tactics by the same actor are divided into separate lines of data. Events are also disaggregated by day. So, for instance, a strike continuing for 10 days is coded as 10 separate "event-days" with unique information for each day coded as available. The purpose of this disaggregation is to move beyond potentially problematic definitions of "event" which inconsistently aggregate disparate actions.

The full sample of events from NAVCO 3.0 includes all physical actions[37] by non-government campaigns in 14 countries.[38] Restricting the sample to physical actions using the CAMEO verb code excludes statements for which the question of nonviolent discipline is not relevant. The countries comprising the sample represent a global cross-section of major civil resistance campaigns over the past 25 years, including all of the cases of regime change in the Arab Spring (Egypt, Tunisia and Yemen). The full sample includes 17,892 events, roughly evenly divided between violent and nonviolent, with a relatively small number of "mixed" events that include both violent and nonviolent elements (see Figure 1 on the following page).

---

[37] In technical terms, the sample excludes all events with a first-level verb code of 13 or lower.
[38] The countries used in this monograph are Algeria, Bahrain, Egypt, Kenya, Libya, Madagascar, Mexico, Morocco, Pakistan, Sudan, Tunisia, Ukraine, Uzbekistan and Yemen.

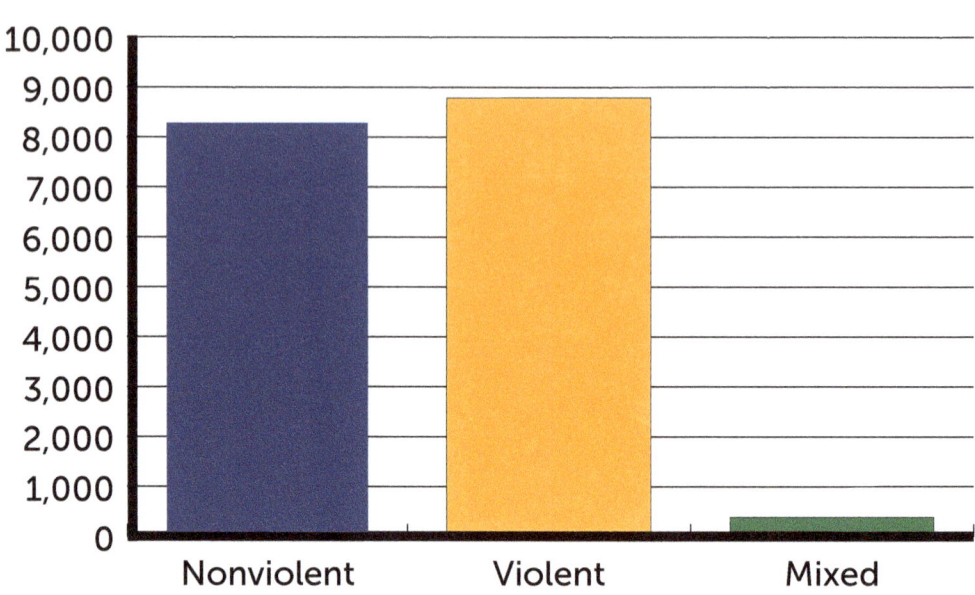

Figure 1. Total Number of Events

Within this sample individual actions were assigned to particular violent or nonviolent campaigns. Assignation followed a two-step process: first, examining data on campaign goals and actor names included in the NAVCO 3.0 data, and second, if necessary, examining the primary sources which informed the data collection to assign the event to a campaign. The definition of campaign used in the assignation process follows Chenoweth and Stephan's definition of a campaign (Chenoweth and Stephan 2011, 6) but relaxes some of their requirements in order to include a larger proportion of events. To be considered a campaign, a group of events had to be meaningfully linked, and have at least three distinct events separated by less than a year.

The overwhelming majority of events were easily and straightforwardly assigned to campaigns following this procedure. The remainder of events where campaign inclusion was more ambiguous were simply coded as "unknown" and dropped from statistical tests where campaign identity was relevant.

Campaigns were then subdivided by several campaign-level variables, including whether the campaign had "maximalist" goals,[39] whether the campaign was primarily violent, and whether the campaign was included in the NAVCO 2.0 dataset. Tests were

---

[39] Maximalist campaigns are defined here as those that seek regime change, secession or an end to occupation. See Chenoweth and Stephan, *Why Civil Resistance Works*.

Statistical Annex

then run variously dropping all events from primarily violent campaigns, dropping events from no campaign, testing only on maximalist campaigns, and testing only on campaigns from NAVCO 2.0. The majority of tests, including all of the results reported in the main text of the monograph, were run dropping events from democracies from the sample. Whether a particular event took place in a democracy was determined using the Polity2 variable from the Polity IV dataset,[40] with events in any country-year with a Polity2 score above 5 considered to be taking place in democracies.

The key dependent variable to measure nonviolent discipline relied on the tactical_choice variable from the NAVCO 3.0 data, which codes whether an event was "nonviolent," "violent," or "mixed." This variable was transformed into a binary variable (nv_discipline) which took a value of 1 if the event was nonviolent, and a value of 0 if the event was violent or "mixed."

A variety of variables from NAVCO 2.0, NAVCO 3.0, and outside datasets were used to operationalize the independent variables. Data on historical experiences of violent and nonviolent resistance came from the NAVCO 2.0 dataset as well as ongoing additions to NAVCO 2.0 being currently coded. Four binary variables: nv_past_success, nv_past_failure, v_past_success, and v_past_failure captured whether the country had successful or failed campaigns from each of these categories. While no formal time delimitation was added to the definition, NAVCO 2.0 captures campaigns taking place as far back as 1945.

The measurement of the availability of a wide range of civil resistance tactics (repertoires of contention) was done using a transformation of NAVCO 3.0's own data. The primary measure of repertoires summed all of the nonviolent actions in a particular year and multiplied that number by the number of types of nonviolent action (captured by the differing CAMEO verbs). This number was then averaged for a five-year period and normalized to a 0 to 1 scale.[41] This measure is the best possible operationalization of repertoires of contention using the NAVCO 3.0 data for several reasons. First, capturing the number of events and multiplying by the number of forms of contention captures the importance of civil resistance being both widespread and consisting of diverse

---

[40] Monty G. Marshall, The Polity IV Annual Time-Series 1800-2014, Dataset (2015), http://www.systemicpeace.org/inscr/p4v2014.xls.
[41] Robustness checks were also using an operationalization of the repertoire score averaged over three years instead of five years, and one which simply summed the number of nonviolent actions and averaged them over five years, skipping the step of multiplying by the number of types of nonviolent actions. Neither of these differing operationalizations significantly changes the result.

tactics. Second, the long-term averaging captures the fact that repertoires change slowly. An even longer average might be preferable, but its feasibility is limited based on the relatively short time span of the NAVCO 3.0 data.

For the external political environment/political opportunity structure (H4) and for repression (H12) testing used the NAVCO 3.0 variable st_posture which captures the state response to a particular event, ranging from full concessions to violent repression with the intent to kill. This variable was used to create binary repress and concessions variables. These two variables were then averaged out over 25 past nonviolent or violent events, giving a rough measure of the number of violent and nonviolent events in the recent past either being repressed or receiving some form of concessions.[42]

The measure of moderate strategic goals was based on a hand-coded "maximalist" variable, informed by NAVCO 3.0's camp_goals variable. These were by hand rather than simply aggregating NAVCO 3.0's original coding, primarily because of missing data issues, as well as to better capture the connections between events.

To measure confrontational/non-confrontational tactical choices, the monograph uses NAVCO 3.0's nv_categ variable, which separates events into Sharp's three categories of "protest and persuasion," "noncooperation" and "intervention."[43] Following Sharp, the monograph expects tactics of noncooperation to be the least confrontational, while tactics of nonviolent intervention should be the most confrontational.

Both cohesive leadership and campaign diversity are measured using variables from the NAVCO 2.0 dataset, and thus models including these variables were limited to the population of campaigns previously coded in NAVCO 2.0. Cohesive leadership was measured using NAVCO 2.0's camp_conf_intensity and camp_structure variables, the former of which captures the degree of internal conflict in a campaign (with the full range going from "unity" to "active competition between groups with violence"), and the latter of which captures whether the campaign had a centralized, hierarchical structure. Campaign diversity was operationalized by aggregating NAVCO 2.0's nine dimensions of diversity[44] to create a diversity index with scores ranging from 0 to 9.

The length of the campaign was coded by counting the number of days from the

---

[42] The author's primary testing variable used an average of the past 25 nonviolent or violent events. Robustness checks that average over shorter or longer time periods (10 past events or 30 past events) do not significantly change the results.
[43] Sharp, *The Politics of Nonviolent Action*
[44] Gender, age, class, rural-urban, ideology, political party, regional, ethnic and religious.

first recorded event in the campaign to the event in question. The number of days was calculated by subtracting the first date from the date of the current event in Excel. Since the entire range of this variable is quite large (the maximum value observed in the main testing sample is 7456), to make the variable comparable to others in the model, most tests used a scaled version of the variable. Tests were first run with a 0 to 1 scaled version (i.e. the number of days divided by 7456). To avoid potential bias from extremely high-value outliers, tests were also run using a version scaled to make 1 equal to the mean plus 3 standard deviations (3442.25). Both scaled variables generate similar relationships with the dependent variable.

Finally, one aspect of the "membership criteria" hypothesis was tested by measuring whether actions performed by students and youth are more likely to have breakdowns in nonviolent discipline than others. While this does not directly get at the question of membership criteria, it does speak to one major area in which membership criteria are relevant: the inclusion of youth, as discussed above. This test was performed using NAVCO 3.0's actor codes, which include the STU code for actions by students and the YTH code for action by youth.

Summary statistics on all of my major independent and dependent variables in the main testing sample are included in Table 2 on the following page.[45]

---

[45] All events from non-democracies except those from primarily violent campaigns and those from no campaign.

Table 2. Summary Statistics

Variable	Observation	Mean	Std. Dev.	Minimum	Maximum
NV_Discipline	5987	0.860531	0.346464	0	1
Past Repression (NV)	5684	0.134296	0.169879	0	1
Past Concessions (NV)	5684	0.027573	0.060367	0	0.722222
Past Repression (V)	5565	0.409666	0.259576	0	1
Past Concessions (V)	5565	0.003153	0.013291	0	0.181818
Past Successful Campaign (NV)	4853	0.301463	0.458941	0	1
Past Failed Campaign (NV)	4853	0.512261	0.499901	0	1
Past Successful Campaign (V)	4853	0.534721	0.498844	0	1
Past Failed Campaign (V)	4853	48.43215	131.6934	0	1
Hierarchical Campaign	1208	0.024007	0.153133	0	1
Campaign Internal Conflict	1269	0.651694	0.514804	0	2
Campaign Diversity	1269	6.339638	2.828234	2	9
Event Participation (logged)	2713	2.862363	1.280963	0	6.30103
Repertoire Score	5666	0.098575	0.113608	0	0.446442
Maximalist Campaign	5699	0.471837	0.49925	0	1
Protest	5699	0.30286	0.459536	0	1
Intervention	5699	0.143183	0.35029	0	1
Non-Cooperation	5699	0.43376	0.495636	0	1
Student	5699	0.0876	0.2827	0	1
Campaign Days	5987	476.9733	988.4628	0	7456

The primary statistical tool used in testing was multilevel logistic regression. One of the primary problems in analyzing event data from multiple countries/campaigns is that the various observations from the same country or campaign are not independent. Thus, statistical results from simple linear or logistic regression techniques are likely to be spurious. Scholars in conflict research have typically sought to avoid this problem through the use of robust standard errors.[46] Yet while this approach may help avoid some problems of statistical inference, a superior way to capture the multilevel structure of the data is through multilevel data analysis.[47] Multilevel analysis explicitly includes the fact that contexts matter, and almost always improves the fit and predictive power of statistical models. Multilevel analysis has become the standard in political behavior research, but has only recently begun to be used by scholars of peace and conflict.

For several of the variables which emerged as particularly significant, the main text reports marginal effects and predicted probabilities. These were generated using the most extensive model appropriate for the particular independent variable. For instance, for measuring the marginal effects of variables present in the entire main testing sample, the model with the most entire sample variables was used. For measuring the marginal effects of variables present only in the sample of NAVCO 2.1 campaigns (e.g. hierarchy, internal_conflict, and diversity), the full model with all variables excepting the tactical choice variables (for reasons discussed below) was used. Predicted probabilities at differing values of the independent variable of interest were generated with binary variables set at zero and continuous variables set at their mean.

Results and Discussion

The first major result of the analysis is that the data clearly show the necessity of incorporating context into one's statistical tests. As shown in the Figure 2 "caterpillar plot" on the following page, even civil resistance campaigns from NAVCO have radically different average levels of nonviolent discipline, and the variance for several campaigns makes them significantly different from zero.

---

[46] Chenoweth and Stephan, *Why Civil Resistance Works*
[47] See Marco R. Steenbergen and Bradford S. Jones, "Modeling Multilevel Data Structures," *American Journal of Political Science* 46.1 (2002).

The simple lesson may be unsurprising but reinforces the critical importance of using appropriate statistical methods to capture these critical differences.[48]

Figure 2. *Base Likelihood of NVD in NAVCO Campaigns*

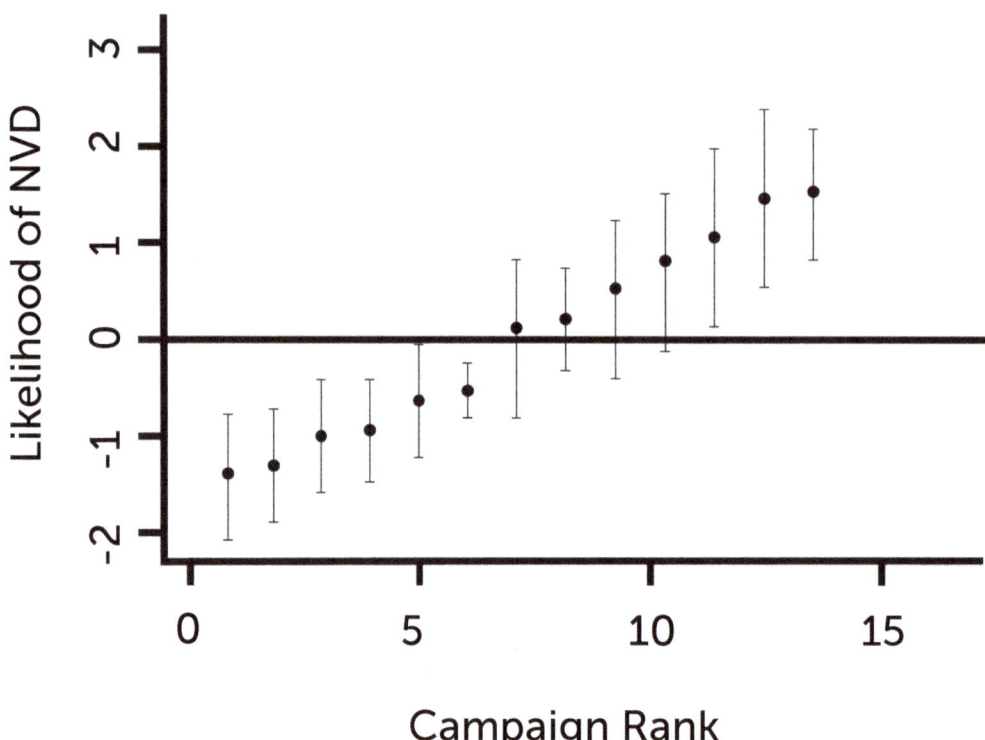

I summarize the main variations on the models in Table 3 on the following page. As shown in the table many of the variables follow their expected sign and significance. Past repression of nonviolent action is one of the most consistent factors reducing nonviolent discipline across models. In almost every constellation of variables, levels of past repression are a substantive and significant predictor of breakdowns in nonviolent discipline.

---

[48] The vertical axis of Figure 2 captures the likelihood of maintaining nonviolent discipline at a particular event for each of the NAVCO campaigns (with no independent variables included in the model), measured in log-odds. The campaigns are ranked from least likely to most likely along the x-axis. The points are the likelihoods themselves while the lines extending from the points represent a 95% confidence interval. Campaigns whose confidence interval does not cross the zero line have a log-odds of maintaining nonviolent discipline significantly different than zero.

Table 3. Regression Models

	Model 1	Model 2	Model 3	Model 4	Model 5	Model 6	Model 7
Past Repression (NV)	-2.556***	-2.447***	-2.656***	-2.473***	-2.649***	-1.574***	-0.645***
Past Concessions (NV)		-5.110***	-5.062***	-5.136***	-5.017***	-9.253***	-21.642***
Past Repression (V)		-0.263	-0.321	-0.200	-0.106	0.730	0.693
Past Concessions (V)		0.327	0.301	0.011	0.898	5.063	8.712
Past Successful Campaign (NV)			-0.114	-0.166	-0.0846	2.339***	2.569*
Past Failed Campaign (NV)			-1.060***	-1.139***	-0.853**	0.314	-0.165
Past Successful Campaign (V)			-0.078	-0.151	-0.232	0.583	1.680
Past Failed Campaign (V)			0.564	0.663	0.567	-1.221**	-3.091**
Repertoire Score				0.218	0.258	-1.313	1.280
Maximalist Campaign				-2.602***	-2.548***		
Student					-0.548***	-0.154	-0.381
Campaign Days (scaled)					-1.025***	1.364	
Hierarchy						-1.174*	1.756
Internal Conflict						1.634**	1.842**
Protest							4.432***
Constant	3.387***	3.644***	3.470***	4.181***	4.245***	0.428	-2.221
n	5978	5855	4929	4755	4755	965	965
n(campaigns)	230	227	198	195	195	10	10
Wald Chi2	64.09***	102.27***	125.18***	150.53***	157.02***	58.42***	236.55***

Surprisingly, however, concessions following past nonviolent actions also significantly reduce nonviolent discipline, and the relationship remains robust across multiple models.[49] This finding, suggesting that breakdowns in nonviolent discipline are more likely following concessions to civil resistance campaigns, runs counter to the logic discussed in the previous section. The finding does not appear to be a statistical artefact, either, remaining robust to alternative specification of the independent variable, or dropping outliers (any observation more than 3 standard deviations from the mean) from the sample. There are a significant number of outliers when it comes to concessions, with 160 observations more than 3 standard deviations higher than the mean. However, while dropping these outliers does slightly reduce the significance of the concessions relationship it does not substantively effect the size of the coefficient or make it statistically insignificant.

Potential rationales for this unexpected relationship, particularly a relaxation of campaign restrictions, are discussed in more detail in the main text.

On their own, the measures of past violent repression and concessions do not have significant effects on levels of nonviolent discipline. However, substituting the separate violent and nonviolent measures of past repression and concessions into a single measure of repression and concessions[50] follows the same pattern as the solely nonviolent measures.

The measures of history have mixed results. In the larger sample of all civil resistance campaigns in non-democracies, none of these variables reach statistical significance. Only the variable measuring a past failed violent campaign approaches significance, and the coefficient is so small that its effect is virtually indistinguishable from zero.

However, this picture changes when the sample is reduced to the events in NAVCO 2.0 campaigns. In this sample, all four variables have their expected effects, with a history of successful nonviolent resistance and failed violent resistance increasing nonviolent discipline and failed nonviolent resistance and successful violent resistance decreasing nonviolent discipline.

The prior use of a wide range of civil resistance tactics (the repertoire of contention) has an unexpected effect – strongly decreasing nonviolent discipline in the larger sample

---

[49] The size of the coefficient, rather than reflecting a great significant impact, reflects the very low mean and standard deviation of the concessions variable. See the summary statistics table.

[50] Equal to the level of violent repression/concessions minus the level of nonviolent repression/concessions.

of civil resistance campaigns, but having no significant effect in the NAVCO campaigns. The student participation variable has a similar effect, reducing nonviolent discipline in the full population of campaigns, but losing statistical significance in the NAVCO campaigns.

All of the campaign attribute variables (hierarchy, internal conflict and diversity) are only available for the NAVCO campaigns, and thus all of the tests are limited to that smaller population of events. The diversity score never comes close to statistical significance, with very high p values in every version of the model. The variables measuring hierarchy and internal conflict are significant, but their signs are the reverse of the expected relationship, with hierarchy negatively associated with nonviolent discipline and internal conflict positively associated with nonviolent discipline. The potential rationale for this reverse relationship is discussed at some length in the main text. One potential explanation is that nonviolent discipline more closely follows Mattaini's argument for individual ownership and input over the campaign rather than Pearlman's argument about fragmentation.[51]

The duration of the campaign followed the expected relationship in the main testing sample, with breakdowns in nonviolent discipline significantly more likely as the number of days since the beginning of the campaign increased. However, the significance of the variable was inconsistent when limited to the sample of NAVCO 2.0 campaigns, suggesting a less than fully robust relationship.

Finally, the tactical variables provide a complex interpretational picture. While they are highly significant in the full model, further investigation of the data shows this to be largely due to the structure of the data. In contrast to protest, noncooperation and intervention verbs in NAVCO 3.0, which typically describe nonviolent events, several of the other verbs with which they are being compared as a reference are by definition violent. Thus, rather than truly being measured against one another, the tactics are primarily being measured against events such as shootings and riots which are, by definition, violent.

To test whether these relationships held when truly being compared against one another, the same tests were performed while dropping these inherently violent events (which represent the majority of breakdowns in nonviolent discipline in the data) from

---

[51] Mattaini, *Strategic nonviolent Power*, Pearlman, *Palestinian National Movement*.

the dataset. When the population is reduced in this way, the statistical significance of the three types of civil resistance breaks down. However, while the pattern is unstable, protests and noncooperation do tend to be positively related to nonviolent discipline, while intervention is slightly negatively related to it.

The findings of the statistical research are briefly summarized in table 5 on the following page, while the implications of the findings are discussed in detail in the main text.

Table 4. Statistical Results

	Independent Variable	Testing Results
H1	Historical Experience of Violent and Nonviolent Contention	Supported
H2	Information on Civil Resistance Campaigns	Not Tested
H3	Nonviolent Repertoire of Contention	Not Supported
H4	Political Opportunity Structure Rewarding Nonviolent Action	Reverse Relationship
H5	Appeals from Movement Leaders for Nonviolent Discipline	Not Tested
H6	Strong, Cohesive Campaign Leadership	Reverse Relationship
H7	Moderate Strategic Goals	Supported
H8	Tactical Choices to Avoid Confrontation	Unclear
H9	Membership Criteria Excluding Violent Actors	Unclear
H10	High Levels of Diversity	Not Supported
H11	Campaign Sanctions for Violent Actions	Not Tested
H12	Discriminate Repression of Violent Resistance	Supported
H13	Duration of Campaign	Supported

Cited Literature

Ackerman, Peter, and Berel Rodal. "The Strategic Dimensions of Civil Resistance." *Survival* 50, no. 3 (2008): 111-26.

Ackerman, Peter, and Christopher Kruegler. *Strategic Nonviolent Conflict: The Dynamics of People Power in the 20th Century*. Westport, CT: Praeger Publishers, 1993.

Ackerman, Peter, and Jack DuVall. *A Force More Powerful: A Century of Nonviolent Conflict*. New York, NY: Palgrave, 2000.

—. "The Right to Rise Up: People Power and the Virtues of Civic Disruption." *The Fletcher Forum of World Affairs* 30, no. 2 (2006): 33-42.

Asal, Victor, Richard Legault, Ora Szekely, and Jonathan Wilkenfeld. "Gender Ideologies and Forms of Contentious Mobilization in the Middle East." *Journal of Peace Research* 50, no. 3 (2013): 305-18.

Bakke, Kristin M. "The Turn to Violence in Self-Determination Struggles in Chechnya and Punjab." In Erica Chenoweth and Adria Lawrence, eds. *Rethinking Violence: States and Non-State Actors in Conflict*. Cambridge, MA: MIT Press, 2010, pp. 221-48.

Bartkowski, Maciej J., ed. *Recovering Nonviolent History: Civil Resistance in Liberation Struggles*. Boulder, CO: Lynne Reiner Publishers, 2013.

Bartkowski Maciej, and Julia Taleb. "Myopia of the Syrian Struggle and Key Lessons," In Mathew Burrows and Maria Stephan (ed.) *Is Authoritarianism Staging a Comeback?* Washington, DC: Atlantic Council Publication, 2015.

Batstone, Jade. "The Use of Strategic Nonviolent Action in the Arab Spring." *Peace Review* 26, no. 1 (2014): 28-37.

Beyerle, Shaazka M. *Curtailing Corruption: People Power for Accountability and Justice*. Boulder, CO: Lynne Reiner Publishers, 2014.

Bond, Douglas G. "The Nature and Meanings of Nonviolent Direct Action: An Exploratory Study." *Journal of Peace Research* 25, no. 1 (1988): 81-89.

Boserup, Anders, and Andrew Mack. *War Without Weapons: Non-Violence in National Defense*. New York, NY: Schocken Books, 1974.

Braithwaite, Alex, Jessica Maves Braithwaite, and Jeffrey Kucik. "The Conditioning Effect of Protest History on the Emulation of Nonviolent Conflict." *Journal of Peace Research* 52, no. 6 (2015): 697-711.

Burrowes, Robert J. *The Strategy of Nonviolent Defense: A Gandhian Approach*. Albany,

NY: State University of New York Press, 1996.

Burrows, Mathew and Maria J. Stephan, eds. *Is Authoritarianism Staging a Comeback?* Washington, DC: The Atlantic Council, 2015.

Butcher, Charles R., and Isak Svensson. "Manufacturing Dissent: Modernization and the Onset of Major Nonviolent Resistance Campaigns." *Journal of Conflict Resolution,* 2014.

Canon, Gabrielle, and Bryan Schatz. " 'Black Lives Matter' Aspires to Reclaim the Legacy of Martin Luther King Jr." *Mother Jones* (January 18, 2015). Accessed 1/30/15 at http://www.motherjones.com/politics/2015/01/black-lives-matter-martin-luther-king-day-civil-rights-protests.

Chenoweth, Erica. *Nonviolence and Violent Campaigns and Outcomes (NAVCO) Data Project Version 2.1 Codebook*. Denver, CO: Josef Korbel School of International Studies, 2015.

Chenoweth, Erica, and Jay Ulfelder. "Can Structural Conditions Explain the Onset of Nonviolent Uprisings?" *Journal of Conflict Resolution*, 2015: 1-27.

Chenoweth, Erica; Jonathan Pinckney, and Orion Lewis. "Days of Rage: introducing the NAVCO 3.0 Data." Working Paper. 2016.

Chenoweth, Erica, and Kurt Schock. "Do Contemporaneous Armed Challenges Affect the Outcome of Mass Nonviolent Campaigns?" *Mobilization* 20, no. 3 (2015): 1-25.

Chenoweth, Erica, and Maria Stephan. *Why Civil Resistance Works: The Strategic Logic of Nonviolent Conflict*. New York, NY: Columbia University Press, 2011.

Chenoweth, Erica, and Orion Lewis. "Unpacking Nonviolent Campaigns: Introducing the NAVCO 2.0 Data." *Journal of Peace Research* 50, no. 3 (2013): 415-23.

Clements, Kevin P. "Principled Nonviolence: An Imperative, Not an Optional Extra." *Asian Journal of Peacebuilding* 3, no. 1 (2015): 1-17.

Codur, Anne-Marie, and Mary Elizabeth King. "Women and Civil Resistance," in *Women, War and Violence: Topography, Resistance and Hope*, vol. 2, ed. Lester R. Kurtz and Mariam M. Kurtz. Santa Barbara, CA: Praeger Publishing, Inc., 2014.

Cunningham, Kathleen G., "Understanding Strategic Choice: The Determinants of Civil War and Nonviolent Campaigns in Self-Determination Disputes." *Journal of Peace Research* 50, no. 3 (2013): 291-304.

—. "Actor Fragmentation and Civil War Bargaining: How Internal Divisions Generate Civil Conflict." *American Journal of Political Science* 57, no. 3 (2013): 659-72.

—. *Inside the Politics of Self-Determination*. New York, NY: Oxford University Press, 2014.

Cunningham, Kathleen G. and Emily Beaulieu. "Dissent, Repression, and Inconsistency." In Erica Chenoweth and Adria Lawrence, ed. *Rethinking Violence: States and Non-State Actors in Conflict*. Cambridge, MA: MIT Press, 2010.

Day, Elizabeth. "#BlackLivesMatter: The Birth of a New Civil Rights Movement." *The Guardian* (July 19, 2015). Accessed 1/30/15 at http://www.theguardian.com/world/2015/jul/19/blacklivesmatter-birth-civil-rights-movement.

Day, Joel, Jonathan Pinckney, and Erica Chenoweth. "Collecting Data on Nonviolent Action: Lessons Learned and Ways Forward." *Journal of Peace Research* 52, no. 1 (2015): 129-33.

Galtung, Johan. "Violence, Peace, and Peace Research." *Journal of Peace Research* 6, no. 3 (1969): 167-91.

Gandhi, Mohandas K. *The Collected Works of Mahatma Gandhi*, Vols 1-98. New Delhi, India: Publications Division Government of India, 1999.

Garrow, David J. *Bearing the Cross: Martin Luther King Jr., and the Southern Christian Leadership Conference*. New York, NY: Perennial Classics, 1986.

George, Alexander L., and Andrew Bennett. *Case Studies and Theory Development in the Social Sciences*. Cambridge, MA: MIT Press, 2005.

Gleditsch, Kristian Skrede and Mauricio Rivera. "The Diffusion of Nonviolent Campaigns." *Journal of Conflict Resolution* (online), 2015.

Gregg, Richard B. *The Power of Non-Violence*. London, UK: George Routledge and Sons, 1935.

Hallward, Maia Carter. *Transnational Activism and the Israeli-Palestinian Conflict*. New York, NY: Palgrave Macmillan, 2013.

Helvey, Robert. *On Strategic Nonviolent Conflict: Thinking About The Fundamentals*. Boston, MA: The Albert Einstein Institution, 2004.

Hess, David, and Brian Martin. "Repression, Backfire, and the Theory of Transformative Events." *Mobilization* 11, no. 1 (2006): 249-267.

Howes, Dustin Ells. "The Failure of Pacifism and the Success of Nonviolence." *Perspectives on Politics* 11, no. 2 (2013): 427-46.

Isaac, Larry W., Daniel B. Cornfield, Dennis C. Dickerson, James M. Lawson, and Jonathan S. Colet. "'Movement Schools' and the Diffusion of Nonviolent Praxis: Nashville Workshops in the Southern Civil Rights Movement." In Sharon Erickson Nepstad and Lester R. Kurtz, ed. *Nonviolent Conflict and Civil Resistance (Research in Social*

Iyer, Raghavan N. *The Moral and Political Thought of Mahatma Gandhi*. New York, NY: Oxford University Press, 1973.

King Jr., Martin Luther. "The Power of Non-Violence," Lecture, University of California, Berkely, CA, June 4, 1957. Accessed 4/1/16 from http://www.thekingcenter.org/archive/document/power-nonviolence#.

King, Mary Elizabeth. "A Note About Jiu-Jitsu." In *Mahatma Gandhi and Martin Luther King, Jr. The Power of Nonviolent Action*, 2nd edition. New Delhi, India: Indian Council for Cultural Relations and Mehta Publishers, 2002.

—. *A Quiet Revolution: The First Palestinian Intifada and Nonviolent Resistance*. New York, NY: Nation Books, 2009.

—. *Gandhian Nonviolent Struggle and Untouchability in South India: The 1924-25 Vykom Satyagraha and the Mechanisms of Change*. New York, NY: Oxford University Press, 2014.

Kitschelt, Herbert P. "Political Opportunity Structures and Political Protest: Anti-Nuclear Movements in Four Democracies." *British Journal of Political Science* 16, no. 1 (1986): 57-85.

Lawrence, Adria. "Driven to Arms? The Escalation of Violence in Nationalist Conflicts." In Erica Chenoweth and Adria Lawrence, eds. *Rethinking Violence: States and Non-State Actors in Conflict*. Cambridge, MA: MIT Press, 2010, pp. 143-172.

Lichbach, Mark Irving. *The Rebel's Dilemma*. Ann Arbor, MI: University of Michigan Press, 1995.

—. "Deterrence or Escalation? The Puzzle of Aggregate Studies of Repression and Dissent." *Journal of Conflict Resolution* 31, no. 2 (1987): 266-98.

Marshall, Monty G. The Polity IV Annual Time-Series, 1800-2014, Dataset. 2015. http://www.systemicpeace.org/inscr/p4v2014.xls (accessed November 24, 2015).

Martin, Brian. *Justice Ignited: The Dynamics of Backfire*. Lanham, MD: Rowman and Littlefield, 2007.

Martinez, Mario Lopez. "Nonviolence in Social Sciences: Towards a Consensual Definition." *Revista de Paz y Conflictos* 8, no. 1 (2015): 63-81.

Mattaini, Mark. *Strategic Nonviolent Power: The Science of Satyagraha*. Edmonton: Athabasca University Press, 2013.

May, Todd. *Nonviolent Resistance: A Philosophical Introduction*. Malden, MA: Polity

Press, 2015.

McAdam, Doug. *Political Process and the Development of Black Insurgency*, 1930-1970. Chicago, IL: University of Chicago Press, 2010.

McAllister, Pam. *You Can't Kill the Spirit: Stories of Women and Non-Violent Action*. Philadelphia, PA: New Society Publishers, 1988.

McDermott, Rose, Chris Dawes, Elizabeth Prom-Wormley, Lindon Eaves, and Peter K. Hatemi. "MAOA and Aggression: A Gene-Environment Interaction in Two Populations." *Journal of Conflict Resolution* 57, no. 6 (2013): 1043-64.

Mill, John Stuart. *A System of Logic: Rationcinative and Inductive*, Vol 1. London: Parker, 1856.

Moore, Will H. "Repression and Dissent: Substitution, Context, and Timing." *American Journal of Political Science* 42, no. 3 (1998): 851-73.

Nepstad, Sharon Erickson. *Nonviolent Revolutions: Civil Resistance in the Late 20th Century*. Oxford, England: Oxford University Press, 2011.

—. *Nonviolent Struggle: Theories, Strategies, & Dynamics*. New York, NY: Oxford University Press, 2015.

Pearlman, Wendy. *Violence, Nonviolence, and the Palestinian National Movement*. Cambridge, UK: Cambridge University Press, 2011.

Popovic, Srdja, Slobodan Djinovic, Andrej Miliojevic, Hardy Merriman, and Ivan Marovic. *CANVAS Core Curriculum: A Guide to Effective Nonviolent Struggle*. Belgrade, Serbia: Center for Applied Nonviolent Action and Strategies, 2007.

Riker, William H. "The Political Psychology of Rational Choice Theory." *Political Psychology* 16, no. 1 (1995): 23-44.

Roberts, Adam, and Timothy Garton Ash. *Civil Resistance and Power Politics: The Experience of Non-Violent Action from Gandhi to the Present*. Oxford, England: Oxford University Press, 2009.

Schock, Kurt. *Unarmed Insurrections: People Power Movements in Nondemocracies*. Minneapolis, MN: University of Minnesota Press, 2005.

—. *Civil Resistance Today*. Malden, MA: Polity Press, 2015.

Schrodt, Philip A. "CAMEO: Conflict and Mediation Event Observations Event and Actor Codebook." Computational Event Data System. March 2012. http://eventdata.parusanalytics.com/cameo.dir/CAMEO.Manual.1.1b3.pdf (accessed November 22, 2015).

Sharp, Gene. *The Political Equivalent of War: Civil Defence*. New York, NY: Carnegie

Endowment for International Peace, 1965.

—. *The Politics of Nonviolent Action*. Boston, MA: Porter Sargent Publishers, Inc., 1973.

—. *Gandhi as Political Strategist: With Essays on Ethics and Politics*. Boston, MA: Porter Sargent Publishers, Inc, 1979.

—. "Nonviolent Action." In Lester R. Kurtz and Jennifer E. Turpin, *Encyclopedia of Violence, Peace, and Conflict*, vol. 2. San Diego, CA: Academic Press, 1999.

—. *Waging Nonviolent Struggle: 20th Century Practice and 21st Century Potential*. Boston, MA: Porter Sargent Publishers, Inc., 2005.

Shridharani, Krishnalal. *War Without Violence: A Study of Gandhi's Method and Its Accomplishments*. New York, NY: Harcourt Brace, 1939.

Sorensen, Majken Jul, and Stellan Vinthagen. "Nonviolent Resistance and Culture." *Peace & Change* 37, no. 3 (2012): 444-70.

Steenbergen, Marco R., and Bradford S. Jones. "Modeling Multilevel Data Structures." *American Journal of Political Science* 46, no. 1 (2002): 218-37.

Stephan, Maria. "Fighting for Statehood: The Role of Civilian-Based Resistance in the East Timorese, Palestinian, and Kosovo Albanian Self-Determination Movements." *Fletcher Forum For World Affairs* 30, no. 2 (2006): 57-79.

Summy, Ralph. "Nonviolence and the Case of the Extremely Ruthless Opponent." *Global Change, Peace & Security* 6, no. 1 (1994): 1-29.

Sutton, Jonathan, Charles R. Butcher, and Isak Svensson. "Explaining Political Jiu-Jitsu: Institution-Building and the Outcomes of Regime Violence Against Unarmed Protests." *Journal of Peace Research* 51, no. 5 (2014): 559-73.

Tarrow, Sidney. "Cycles of Collective Action: Between Moments of Madness and the Repertoire of Contention." *Social Science History* 17, no. 2 (1993): 281-307.

—. *Power in Movement: Social Movements and Contentious Politics*. Cambridge, England: Cambridge University Press, 1998.

Tilly, Charles. *From Mobilization to Revolution*. Reading, MA: Addison Wesley Publishing Company, 1978.

Weber, Thomas. " 'The Marchers Simply Walked Forward Until Struck Down:' Nonviolent Suffering and Conversion." *Peace & Change* 18, no. 3 (1993): 267-89.

White, Peter B., Dragana Vidovic, Belen Gonzalez, Kristian Skrede Gleditsch, and David E. Cunningham. "Nonviolence as a Weapon of the Resourceful: From Claims to Tactics in Mobilizations." *Mobilization: An International Quarterly* 20, no. 4 (2015): 471-91.

Wood, Elisabeth Jean. *Insurgent Collective Action and Civil War in El Salvador*. Cambridge, UK: Cambridge University Press, 2003.

Zunes, Stephen. "Unarmed Insurrections Against Authoritarian Governments in the Third World: A New Kind of Revolution." *Third World Quarterly*, 1994: 403-26.

—. "The Role of Non-Violent Action in the Downfall of Apartheid." *The Journal of Modern African Studies* 37, no. 1 (1999): 137-69.

Zunes, Stephen, Lester R. Kurtz, and Sarah Beth Asher. *Nonviolent Social Movements: A Geographical Perspective*. Malden, MA: Blackwell Publishers, 1999.

Case Study References

In addition to the sources below, the author conducted a general review of all of the articles from various news sources during the peak periods of the campaigns in question. My sources were *Agence France Presse – English*, *The New York Times*, *The Guardian*, *The Wall Street Journal*, and the *Christian Science Monitor*. For Serbia I ran the search for September 24, 2000 through October 5, 2000. For Georgia I ran the search for November 1, 2003 through November 24, 2003. For Kyrgyzstan I ran the search for February 1, 2005 through March 24, 2005.

Anjaparidze, Zaal. "Georgian Advisors Stepping Forward in Bishkek." *Eurasia Daily Monitor*, March 24, 2005.

Beissinger, Mark. "Structure and Example in Modular Political Phenomena: The Diffusion of Bulldozer/Rose/Orange/Tulip Revolutions." *Perspectives on Politics* 5, no. 2 (2007): 259-76.

Binnendijk, Anika Locke, and Ivan Marovic. "Power and Persuasion: Nonviolent Strategies to Influence State Security Forces in Serbia (2000) and Ukraine (2004)." *Communist and Post-Communist Studies* 39, no. 3 (2006): 411-29.

Bujosevic, Dragan, and Ivan Radovanovic. *The Fall of Milosevic: The October 5th Revolution*. New York: Palgrave Macmillan, 2003.

Bunce, Valerie J., and Sharon L. Wolchik. Defeating Authoritarian Leaders in Postcommunist Countries. Cambridge, England: Cambridge University Press, 2011.

Fairbanks, Charles. "Georgia's Rose Revolution." Journal of Democracy 15, no. 2 (2004): 110-24.

Finn, Peter. "Kyrgyz Protesters Seize Sites in South: Growing Anti-Government Unrest Follows Charges of Recent Electoral Fraud." The Washington Post, March 22, 2005: A12.

Fuhrmann, Matthew. "A Tale of Two Social Capitals: Revolutionary Collective Action in Kyrgyzstan." Problems of Post-Communism 53, no. 6 (2006): 16-29.

Huskey, Eugene. "Kyrgyzstan's Tulip Revolution: Interview with Roza Otunbayeva." Demokratizatsiya 13, no. 4 (2005): 483-9.

International Crisis Group. "Kyrgyzstan: After the Revolution." ICG. May 4, 2005. http://

www.crisisgroup.org/~/media/Files/asia/central-asia/kyrgyzstan/097_kyrgyzstan_after_the_revolution.pdf (accessed November 29, 2015).

Jakopovich, Dan. "The 2003 `Rose Revolution'" in Georgia: A Case Study in High Politics and Rank-and-File Execution." *Journal of Contemporary Central and Eastern Europe* 15, no. 2 (2007): 211-20.

Jones, Kevin Dewitt. The Dynamics of Political Protests: A Case Study of the Kyrgyz Republic. College Park, MD: University of Maryland Unpublished Dissertation, 2007.

Kandelaki, Giorgi. *Georgia's Rose Revolution: A Participant's Perspective*. Washington, DC: United States Institute of Peace, 2006.

Kimmage, Daniel. "Kyrgyzstan: How Bishkek's Revolution Happened So Fast." *Radio Free Europe/Radio Liberty*. April 4, 2005. http://www.rferl.org/content/article/1058253.html (accessed November 15, 2015).

Kulov, Emir. "March 2005: Parliamentary Elections as a Catalyst of Protests." *Central Asian Survey* 27, no. 3 (2008): 337-47.

Marat, Erica. The Tulip Revolution: Kyrgyzstan One Year After. Washington, DC: The Jamestown Foundation, 2006.

Meyers, Nancy L. *Vreme Je! It's Time! Mobilization and Voting for Regime Change: The Serbian Elections of 2000*. Washington, DC: Unpublished Dissertation, The George Washington University, 2009.

Mitchell, Lincoln. "Georgia's Rose Revolution." *Current History* 103 (October 2004): 342-8.

Mydans, Seth. "President of Georgia Pleads for Calm as Protests Grow." *The New York Times*, November 15, 2003: A1.

Nodia, Ghia. "The Dynamics and Sustainability of the Rose Revolution." In *Democratisation in the European Neighborhood*, edited by Michael Emerson, 38-52. Brussels: Centre for European Policy Studies, 2005.

Peuch, Jean-Christophe. "Kyrgyzstan: Eyewitness to the Revolution." *Radio Free Europe/Radio Liberty*. March 25, 2005. http://www.rferl.org/content/article/1058136.html (accessed November 15, 2015).

Radnitz, Scott. *Weapons of the Wealthy: Predatory Regimes and Elite-Led Protests in Central Asia*. Ithaca: Cornell University Press, 2010.

Vejvoa, Ivan. "Civil Society versus Slobodan Milosevic: Serbia, 1991-2000." In *Civil Resistance & Power Politics: The Experience of Non-Violent Action from Gandhi to the Present*, eds. Adam Roberts and Timothy Garton Ash. Oxford: Oxford University Press, 2009.

Walsh, Nick Paton. "Kyrgyz Leader Condemns Protesters." *The Guardian*, March 22, 2005 (a).

—. "Pink Revolution Rumbles on in Blood and Fury." The Guardian, March 26, 2005 (b).

Wood, Tom. "Reflections on the Revolution in Kyrgyzstan." *Fletcher Forum on World Affairs* 30, no. 2 (2006): 43-56.

List of Tables and Figures

Fig. 1. Nonviolent Discipline Spectrum 17
Tab. 1. Mathematical Model Elements 23
Tab. 2. Expected Influences for Testing 33
Fig. 2. Illustrating Past Repression Influence 36
Fig. 3. Percentage of Actions Repressed 37
Fig. 4. Effects of Repression on Nonviolent Discipline 38
Fig. 5. Campaign Structure and Likelihood of Maintaining Nonviolent Discipline 40
Fig. 6. Strategic Goals and Likelihood of Maintaining Nonviolent Discipline 42
Tab. 3. Results of Statistical Analysis 44
Tab. 4. Color Revolution Comparison Snapshot 46
Map of Serbia 48
Map of Georgia 52
Map of Kyrgyzstan 55
Tab. 5. Main Findings from Case Comparison 58
Tab. 6. Case Comparison and Statistics Findings 67
Appendix Tab. 1. Case Comparison and Statistics Findings 77
Appendix Fig. 1. Total Number of Events 78
Appendix Tab. 2. Summary Statistics 82
Appendix Fig. 2. Base Likelihood of NVD in NAVCO Campaigns 84
Appendix Tab. 3. Regression Models 85
Appendix Tab. 4. Statistical Results 89

www.ingramcontent.com/pod-product-compliance
Lightning Source LLC
Chambersburg PA
CBHW041646040426
R18086900002B/R180869PG42333CBX00016B/7